Best iPhone Apps

Second Edition

The Guide for Discriminating Downloaders

J.D. Biersdorfer

Köln · Sebastopol · Tokyo

Best iPhone Apps, Second Edition: The Guide for Discriminating Downloaders
by J.D. Biersdorfer

Published by O'Reilly Media, Inc., 1005 Gravenstein Highway North, Sebastopol, CA 95472.

O'Reilly books may be purchased for educational, business, or sales promotional use. Online editions are also available for most titles (*http://my.safaribooksonline.com*). For more information, contact our corporate/institutional sales department: (800) 998-9938 or *corporate@oreilly.com*.

Editor: Peter McKie	**Cover Design:** Monica Kamsvaag
Production Editor: Nellie McKesson	**Interior Design:** Josh Clark, Edie Freedman, and Nellie McKesson
Indexer: Julie Hawks	

Printing History:
 First Edition: October 2009
 Second Edition: September 2010

ISBN: 978-1-449-39414-1

[TI]

Contents

Contents

Foreword

When the first edition of this book appeared in the summer of 2009, Apple's App Store offered around 50,000 mini-programs. Little more than a year later, the App Store has passed the 250,000 mark and is blazing a trail toward a 300,000 apps. With all of them clamoring for your attention, how do you know which ones rise above the others and which ones you should avoid like day-old sushi in a heat wave?

You could trawl the App Store for new releases every week, listen to Apple's Genius suggestions, or poll iPhone- and iPod Touch-owning friends. Or you could get a book like the one you're holding, the brand-new edition of *Best iPhone Apps*.

So what does it mean to be the "best"? If you think about it, *best* really is a loaded word. Its usage lurches between something you can prove (as in, "*Toy Story 3* had the best ticket sales of any movie opening this weekend") and something that's a matter of personal or collective opinion (as in, "The Oscar for Best Picture goes to…").

A combination of factors came into play when I selected this year's best iPhone apps. The biggest one was copious amounts of time spent in the App Store, downloading and testing hundreds of apps to see how they performed. User interface was also a consideration—was the app easy to use and navigate, or did it seem like it was designed by the Galactic Avengers from Planet Garble? And yes, even some personal opinion went into the decision-making.

Other aspects of the evaluation process—like overall sales, App Store popularity, professional reviews, and user ratings—held less sway, but couldn't be ignored. After all, when you see that Angry Birds (page 116) is the best-selling game several weeks in a row, gets overwhelmingly rave reviews, and has a devoted fan base around the world, you wonder what all the fuss is about and download the game. (And when the app's sheer inventiveness consumes so much time that it nearly causes the author to miss a deadline, the app tends to get included in *Best iPhone Apps*.)

The seven chapters in this book touch on the major aspects of your daily life, from work to play, and home to travel. So sit back, relax, and take a stroll through the next 200 pages or so. You'll find apps that will change how you use your iDevice—and maybe make you use it more often.

Have fun stormin' the App Store!

About the Author

J.D. Biersdorfer is the author of *iPad: The Missing Manual*, *iPod: The Missing Manual*, *Netbooks: The Missing Manual*, and several other books. She writes for the *New York Times* (a lot); has written for the *AIGA Journal of Graphic Design*, *Budget Travel*, and *Rolling Stone*; and has contributed essays to several books on the collision of technology, art, and pop culture. She got her first iPhone at an AT&T store in Pennsylvania on June 29, 2007, and her current iPhone on June 24, 2010, after standing in line at Apple's West 14th St. store in Manhattan for 6 hours. She welcomes feedback at *jd.biersdorfer@gmail.com*, but suggests contacting the app's developer if you're having a specific problem.

Best Apps For Work

Compared to smartphones favored by big corporations (*cough* *BlackBerry* *cough*), the sleek and shiny iPhone may seem like its main contribution to the workplace is to sit there and look pretty while you wait for your spouse to call. But don't underestimate it. With the right apps, your iPhone becomes a serious tool for running the office (and Microsoft Office) right from your pocket.

This chapter highlights just a fraction of the huge number of apps aimed at people who want to do more than watch tiny movies on the train. They help you **get things done**, like brainstorming ideas and tracking projects.

Your iPhone or iPod Touch also helps you **work on the go**, from editing spreadsheets in a waiting room to taking dictation. Apps can also unclutter your life by converting paper to pixels or the reverse, turning pixels into paper (by printing them).

Communication is key, and apps that **make phone calls** *easier* keep you better connected to your clients and coworkers. And when you really need to get down to business and **geek out**, like control your desktop PC from your phone or update the company blog from your Touch, you can do that, too. Read on to find out how to tap the iPhone's business potential.

Photo: Herval Freire

Best App for Quick To-Do Lists

TaskPaper

$9.99
Version 1.2.4 | Hog Bay Software
For all iPhones and the iPod Touch

There's no shortage of organizer apps for your handheld, but some are more complex than they need to be. Enter TaskPaper, a no-nonsense app for quickly writing down things you need to do. It organizes your reminders into three categories: tasks, projects, and notes. You can manage your lists online at *simpletext.ws*, a free site that stores and syncs TaskPaper notes (you need a Google account to log in and use it).

BLANK SLATE: TaskPaper lets you jot down thoughts in a hurry, without getting bogged down with unnecessary bells and whistles. Type in an item and then tap the gear-shaped icon in the bottom-right to get to basic word-processing commands, apply searchable tags, or to change an item's category. TaskPaper automatically adds bullet points to its task lists.

LEFT AND RIGHT: Swipe your finger from right to left to call up text-editing commands. Swipe left to right across a completed task to knock it off the list. Crossed-off items get an automatic Done tag (@done) so you can see your accomplishments in one place, and you can add your own tags to list items and search for them anytime.

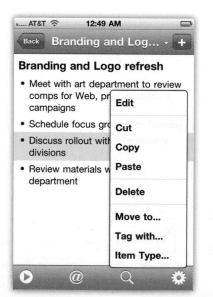

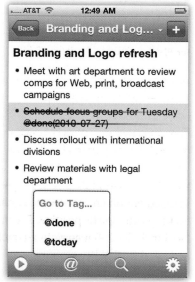

For Work

Best App for Tracking Goals

Touch Goal

$3.99
Version 1.7.2 | Green Onion Software
For all iPhones and the iPod Touch

Setting goals—and working toward them—is often easier if you can see how you're doing along the way. With Touch Goal, you can enter as many professional or personal ambitions as you want—as well as bad habits you want to break—and see your progress mapped out on an easy-to-read graph. To keep your spirits positive, Touch Goal includes 250 inspirational quotes and soothing background images.

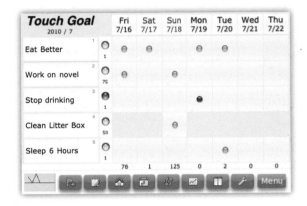

CONNECT THE DOTS: Once you meet a goal (or defeat one of your vices), tap the chart to "check it off." Touch Goal totals your daily score at the bottom of the chart. Tap the buttons along the bottom of the screen to add new goals or to see them entered on a calendar.

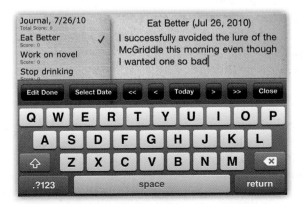

WRITE ON: On the main screen (shown above), tap the note-pad icon to enter your thoughts on a goal in a daily journal. You can review diary entries from specific days by tapping the Select Date button or by advancing (or retreating) through the days with the arrow buttons.

Best App for Sketching Out Ideas

iNapkin
$2.99
Version 1.3 | Luksor
For all iPhones and the iPod Touch

Inspiration can strike at any moment, and cocktail napkins have historically been pressed into service to sketch out visual ideas or jot down quick bits of information (when they're not blotting drink rings, that is). iNapkin brings the same concept to the small screen for people who hate typing on the iPhone's tiny keyboard or who just need to dash off a drawing. Just tap open a fresh napkin, grab your virtual pen, and let your fingers do the talking.

NAP TIME: iNapkin gives you three basic tools: a five-color "pen" for writing, an eraser for corrections, and a hand tool so you can drag different parts of the napkin to the center of your gadget's screen. Drawing efficiently on the 3.5-inch screen may take a bit of experimentation to get the right touch, but there's plenty of napkin to practice on.

PAPER 2.0: With iNapkin, you don't have to worry about losing your scrap of an idea since it's right there on your iPhone or iPod Touch. The app lets you pick one of three napkin sizes to work with: 512 × 512 pixels, 768 × 1,024 pixels or 960 × 960 pixels. You can email your virtual napkin to other people right from the app or share it with your friends via Facebook.

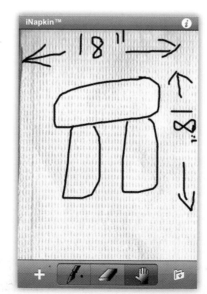

Best App for Sharing Big Files

Dropbox
Free
Version 1.2.4 | Evenflow Inc.
For all iPhones and the iPod Touch

Dropbox gives you a virtual online hard drive you can tap into from anywhere. To use it, sign up for a Dropbox account (prices range from free for 2GB of server space to $20 a month for 100GB). To share files from your desktop computer, install the Dropbox software on your PC or Mac. That puts a Dropbox folder, linked to the Dropbox site, on your desktop. Drag your desktop files into it and access them via the iPhone app.

ONLINE LOCKER: To see a file stored on your Dropbox account, tap the My Dropbox icon and tap the file you want to open. You can read documents, view photos, and watch videos stored there. Dropbox lets you send links by email to others you want to share your files with and you can store photos and videos you capture on your iPhone right in your online Dropbox.

⊕ HONORABLE MENTION

MobileMe iDisk
Free
Version 1.2 | Apple Inc.
For all iPhones and the iPod Touch

Apple's free MobileMe iDisk has many of the same great file-sharing and storage features as Dropbox—with one major difference. While the MobileMe app itself is free, you need a $99-a-year MobileMe subscription to use it. Still, for those with MobileMe accounts (which work on Windows PCs as well as Macs) who sync data and store files online, the free app is a nice perk. You can send download links for big files to friends with just a tap.

5

Best App for Tracking Packages

Delivery Status Touch
$4.99
Version 4.1 | Junecloud LLC
For all iPhones and the iPod Touch

Order a lot of stuff online? Follow those shipments from door to door with this app, which tracks packages sent by more than 25 delivery companies (FedEx, UPS, DHL, even the good ol' US Postal Service) and international post and courier services. You can also track pending orders at e-commerce merchants like Amazon, Apple, Google Checkout, and Adobe before your box even ships.

HAND-DELIVERED: Delivery Status's main screen gives you a quick look at what's on its way and how long it will take to get there. Tap an item for more information, like package contents and a map of the package's current location. With a free *junecloud.com* account, you can enter long tracking numbers on your desktop computer and sync them over to the app.

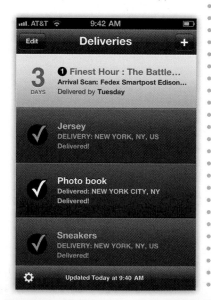

⊕ HONORABLE MENTION

TrackThis
$0.99
Version 1.1 | Fragmented Tech
For all iPhones and the iPod Touch

TrackThis serves the same purpose as Delivery Status Touch: it tells you where your packages are. While the design isn't as polished and it tracks about half as many delivery companies, this app has two major things going for it: It costs just a buck and it includes push notifications to tell you exactly when that new iPhone you ordered has arrived from FedEx. If you order mainly from companies like UPS, FedEx, DHL, or the USPS, this app is just fine.

Best App for Online Productivity

Google Mobile

Free
Version 0.5.6.4029 | Google
For all iPhones and the iPod Touch

Need to dip into Google services while you're on the go? The Big G's own mobile app brings one-stop access to many of its popular online programs, including Gmail, Google Calendar, Google Docs, Google Reader, and Google News. Tap on a service and Safari often pops up to take you there, but you don't have to squint to see the screen—Google Mobile thoughtfully takes you to mobile-friendly versions of all its services.

SPEAK UP: Hate pecking in search terms on the iPhone's tiny keyboard? Tap Google Mobile's microphone icon and speak your keywords into Google Voice Search to get results. You can use many of the famous Google Voice shortcuts, like saying "weather Pensacola" to get the Florida Panhandle forecast or "movies 61615" to see what's playing in Peoria.

OFFICE ONLINE: The free Google Docs service lets you create and share documents, spreadsheets, and presentation files through a web browser. You can edit spreadsheets with a limited set of commands, but other file types are read-only. You can, however, edit them with third-party apps, like DataViz Documents to Go, mentioned later in this chapter.

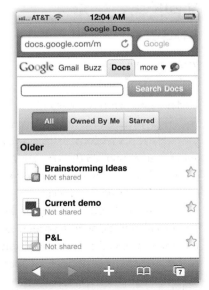

Best App for Digitizing Receipts

TurboScan
Free | $1.99 for full version
Version 1.3 | Pixoft
For all iPhones and the iPod Touch

When it comes time to convert that pocket full of torn and crumpled receipts into electronic files for expense reports and tax records, whip out TurboScan. The iPhone's camera serves as the app's scanner and the app can email receipts as JPEG, PNG, or PDF files; iPod Touch fans can *technically* use the app by importing photos of receipts if you have time but no scanner. The free version scans fully, but imprints digital watermarks on files.

SEEING RED: Place your receipt on a table in decent light and position it so you can get a good snap with the iPhone's camera. When the initial image appears in the TurboScan window, you can adjust the area to be scanned by pushing and pulling the dots on the corner of the red rectangle until you have all the important parts of a document covered.

RECORDS TO GO: One you "scan" a receipt, note, card, or other document, TurboScan quickly processes it into an electronic version that lives on your iPhone. You can leave it there, or email it from the app. For hard-to-read originals, the app offers a SureScan feature that snaps three images of an item, then uses the best one to create the clearest document.

For Work

Best App for Applying to College

CollegeMapp
$1.99
Version 1.0 | CollegeMapp
For all iPhones and the iPod Touch

Created by a college admissions advisor, CollegeMapp brings order to a process that has become increasingly more complicated over the years. The app tracks application deadlines and includes checklists for documents and forms typical of a university application. It also includes links to college websites for admission information. And because you always need a safety school, it tracks the entire process for multiple colleges.

WHATSAMATTA U: Once you set up profiles for all the schools you're applying to, each one gets its own tidy page in College-Mapp. Here, you can record information for each part of the application process. For example, tap Applications to fill in fields for the date you submitted your application, your essay topics, fees paid, and the ID you used on the college's website.

SCHOOL DAZE: While the application maze can feel overwhelming, College-Mapp's checklists keep you on track, including one for financial aid. Once you fill in the app's data fields, tap Send to Email to create a spreadsheet displaying the status of all your applications. You can email it and then print it out to see your progress on paper.

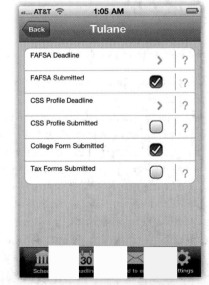

9

Best App for Visual Thinking

iBlueSky
$9.99
Version 2.11| Tenero Software Ltd.
For all iPhones and the iPod Touch

Imagine letting your mind wander around in a brainstorm—while you sketch it all out in a non-linear way. Popular on conference-room whiteboards, these "mind maps" shrink conveniently down to pocket size thanks to iBlueSky. The app lets you create vast, detailed mind maps wherever you happen to be and you can import existing mind maps created in the specialized Novamind, Freemind, and OPML mind-map formats.

IDEA CENTRAL: A mind map starts with a main keyword in the middle of the screen. When you start a new project, the app plants you in this lonely circle and you branch off from there by adding related words, tasks, and projects. Depending on the project, mind maps can get rather large, but iBlueSky can create a giant page 1,500 times larger than your handheld screen.

BRANCHING OUT: Mind maps are basically visual outlines and a graphical way to take notes. As you spin off the central idea, tap the **+** button on the app's main toolbar to add a node or branch. The keyboard slides up so you can type in a label or thought. You can also go back and edit existing text in the map as you refine your ideas—and you don't even need a whiteboard dry eraser.

For Work

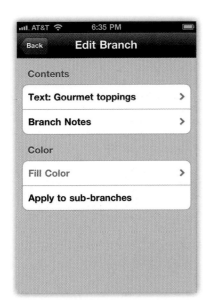

COLOR-CODED: Traditional mind maps use color to signify certain branches sprouting from a main idea and to make the map more visually stimulating. If you don't like the default colors the app uses for your branches, tap an item and then tap the Edit button. Here, you can pick your own colors, add notes about the selected branch, and edit the branch label.

⊕ **HONORABLE MENTION**

MindNode
$5.99
Version 1.2.3 | Markus Müeller
For all iPhones and the iPod Touch

Not quite as graphically elegant as iBlueSky, MindNode might be a bit more intuitive for newbie mindmappers. The work area automatically expands as the mind map grows and you can easily cut, copy, and paste your nodes all over the screen as you branch out from a central idea. MindNode can export and email maps in its own format for the Mac, or as a Freemind or OPML file, or as text. You can also save mind maps as PNG images and import them into other programs.

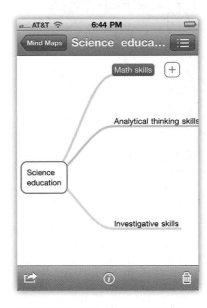

SEEING RED: Start with your main idea, or "super node," and add new nodes by tapping the plus sign and typing in labels as you map out your thoughts. Although mind maps are meant to be sprawling visual representations of an idea, MindNode also lets you see things in a more linear view. Tap the ▤ button to see the nodes listed in vertical outline form.

11

Best App for Working on MS Office Files

Documents to Go
$9.99 | $14.99 for full version
Version 3.3.1 | DataViz Inc.
For all iPhones and the iPod Touch

Microsoft Office is still the king of the business world and Documents to Go has been wrangling Office files on handhelds for years. The app offers a slew of editing features for Word and Excel files; the Premium version lets you edit PowerPoint presentations, too, and sync with online services like Google Docs, Dropbox, Box.net, and iDisk. Both versions are universal, so customers who also own an iPad don't have to buy the app twice.

CELL BLOCK: Documents to Go can both create and edit spreadsheets in Excel 2007, 2008, and 2010, and retain the original formatting when you open and edit the file on your iPhone or iPod Touch. In addition to plenty of cell and row formatting controls, the app offers 111 functions for spreadsheet jockeys and can handle multiple worksheets.

OPEN ALL NIGHT: You can view and edit Word documents attached to email messages right in Documents to Go. The app displays text formatting, plus embedded graphics, tables, and comments. Both the regular and Premium versions also open PowerPoint, PDF, and iWork files, although you can edit PowerPoint presentations only with the Premium edition.

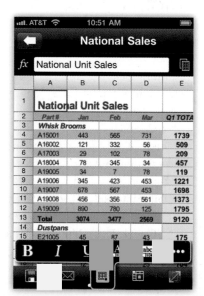

IN SYNC: Documents to Go provides a number of ways to pass documents between handheld and desktop, including email or syncing over a Wi-Fi network with an included desktop app. If you have an iPhone 4 or iOS 4 on your device, you can use iTunes File Sharing to sync documents with the computer when you connect the devices to transfer music, photos, and videos.

Quickoffice Mobile Suite

$4.99 | $9.99 for full version
Version 3.2.0 | Quickoffice Inc.
For all iPhones and the iPod Touch

Running a close second (or perhaps even a tie, if not for DataViz adding PowerPoint editing first), Quickoffice Mobile's $5 app lets you create and edit Word and Excel files and view PowerPoint presentations. The pricier Quickoffice Connect Mobile Suite adds integrated access to online storage services like Dropbox, Google Docs, MobileMe, and Box.net. For more direct copying, both versions can transfer files to a computer over Wi-Fi.

TYPE AND FILE TYPE: Like most apps designed for small screens, Quickoffice Mobile's menu bar keeps the text formatting controls out of the way until you need them. Speaking of formats, along with opening and editing files in Microsoft .doc, .docx, .xls, and .xlsx files, Quickoffice can view iWork attachments, plus HTML files, PDF documents, and several image formats.

Best App for Taking Unique Notes

Evernote
Free
Version 3.3.7 | Evernote
For all iPhones and the iPod Touch

Need to take notes, in all kinds of formats? Evernote lets you take just about any type of note because it records text, audio, and image files (you can even search for text pictured within photos). Evernote is a great standalone app for collecting your thoughts, and you can sync up to 40MB of notes a month at *Evernote.com* or with a free, ad-supported desktop program. Pony up $5 a month for the site's premium service, 500MB of note-sync fun.

NOTA BENE: To get started converting your thoughts into bits and pixels, tap the New Note button and then pick the type of note you wish to create. For images you want to capture as visual notes, take a photo or use one from your photo album (great for those camera-free iPod Touches). Tap the Tips tab for helpful hints on using the app.

SEARCH AND SYNC: Once you start sharing your brain with Evernote, tap the Notes button to see your collected works. You can tag notes of all types with keywords for roundup with a quick search. Tap the star at the top of an open note to mark it as a Favorite. Tap the Sync button to set up your sync options and to log in and out of your *Evernote.com* account.

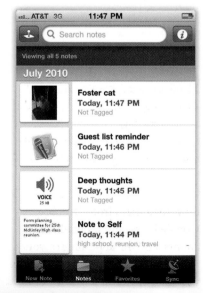

Best App for Reading Documents

ReaddleDocs
$4.99
Version 2.1.7 | Readdle
For all iPhones and the iPod Touch

Electronic documents come in all shapes, sizes, and formats, but odds are ReaddleDocs can crack them open. Microsoft Office documents, eBooks, and large PDF files are no problem for the app. Nor is moving those files around—you can up- and download them from Dropbox, Google Docs, and MobileMe accounts, and the app can turn your handheld into a Wi-Fi flash drive so you can copy files from a PC or Mac.

OFFLINE READING: ReaddleDocs has its own web browser built right in, so there's no need to jump out to Safari if you want to do some online reading. In fact, you can do your online reading offline if you anticipate a lack of Internet access. Tap the Browser button in the app's toolbar, browse to a site, and press the Save button to snag the page for later viewing.

 HONORABLE MENTION

GoodReader
Free | $0.99 for full version
Version 2.8.2 | Good.i.Ware Ltd.
For all iPhones and the iPod Touch

Although it doesn't have the Wi-Fi flash drive feature of ReaddleDocs, GoodReader is a great document viewer in its own right and can display Office, iWork, HTML, audio, and video files. It also handles PDF documents, reflowing the text for the small screen. You can transfer files back and forth over a wireless network connection or through online services like Dropbox and MobileMe. The free Lite version lets you store only five files.

Best App for Scanning Business Cards

ScanBizCards
Free | $6.99 for full version
Version 2.75 | ScanBiz Mobile Solutions
For all iPhones and the iPod Touch

When you have ScanBizCards around, you don't have to worry about losing those little cardboard rectangles that accumulate during your business travels. Just snap a photo of a card with the iPhone's camera (or import a photo into the Touch), and the app scans the card's information right into your contacts list. Older iPhones (pre-3GS) may need a close-up lens attachment for clear images, and the free app only lets you add two cards a week.

CARD READER: To convert a business card into an electronic contact file, snap a clear, well-lit picture of it. The app lets you nudge crooked photos a bit straighter and crop out background clutter. Once you get a good shot, tap the Scan button. After a few seconds of scanning action, the app extracts the card's text into a file you can add to your address book or Outlook contacts.

SCAN PLAN: Check the scanned information and fix any typos that may have occurred from misread smudges or funky fonts. With the full version of the app, you can store card files online via Cloud Sync and see them from any web browser. Tap to send introductory notes to the cardholder, LinkedIn invitations, or to call the number on the card.

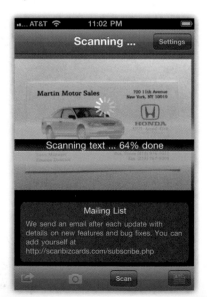

Best App for E-Business Cards

SnapDat

Free
Version 1.4 | SnapDat Networks
For all iPhones and the iPod Touch

If passing out *virtual* business cards appeals to you, consider SnapDat. Using built-in templates, you create your own electronic card (complete with photo) within the app. When you meet other SnapDat users, you exchange your cards by email or over the Snap network—and have the person's details automatically added to your iPhone or iPod contacts. If you like your virtual card, you can get it printed through the app.

MAKING CONTACT: To create your own SnapCard, tap the **+** button on the app's main screen. Tap the Card Design box to choose the visual look of your card. If you have a contact file for yourself in your iPhone or Touch address book, tap the Import from Contacts button to pull in the information. Tap the Edit Contact Info button to choose the fields you want to display.

OH, SNAP: When you want to pass along a card to someone, tap the My SnapCard button on the main screen. A menu pops up giving you several ways to send the card, including as an email attachment to another user's Snap-ID account, or to Facebook and Twitter. Cards sent as email attachments include a .vcf file, a common format for contact lists.

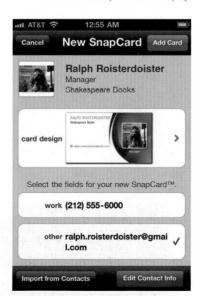

17

Best App for Speaking Your Mind

Dragon Dictation
Free
Version 2.0.0 | Nuance Communications
For all iPhones and the iPod Touch

Secretaries who take dictation are rare and expensive these days, but you can press your iPhone into service for free (or your iPod Touch, with an external microphone). This tap-and-yap app from Nuance is free and uses some of the same speech-recognition technology used by the company's desktop NaturallySpeaking program. At its peak, it can input spoken text about five times faster than fumbling around on a keyboard.

START TALKING: To use Dragon Dictation, press the red recording button in the center of the screen and start speaking clearly into the microphone. You need to have a network connection, and the first time you launch Dragon Dictation, the app politely asks if it can upload the names of your contacts to "improve accuracy," but you can say no.

RECORDING ROOM: As you speak, Dragon Dictation translates your words into text. The app isn't 100% accurate, but you can make corrections through a menu of suggested words or by spoken commands. You can copy and paste finished transcriptions into SMS or email messages, and you can update your Facebook and Twitter status by voice, too.

Best App for Printing

PrintCentral
$7.99
Version 1.5.4 | EuroSmartz Ltd.
For all iPhones and the iPod Touch

If you search the App Store for *printing*, many of the apps that turn up will come from EuroSmartz. These apps print various things, but if you want just one app, PrintCentral packs in the most features. You can print documents, photos, mail messages, contacts, and more to most Wi-Fi printers, print over a 3G/EDGE connection, and even grab files to print from online storage lockers like Dropbox and Google Docs.

RELAY STATION: While PrintCentral prints directly to most printers on Wi-Fi networks, it's not as direct for USB or Bluetooth printers. For starters, you need to download and install EuroSmartz's free WePrint software to your PC or Mac. Once you configure the software, the mobile app bounces the print job from your iPhone to the desktop and then to the printer.

PRINT ON DEMAND: PrintCentral's main screen holds a menu of all the sources you can print from, including your contacts list, stored documents, email messages, and photo albums. PrintCentral also includes its own web browser. When you want to print a web page, point the browser to the site and tap the printer icon in the upper-right corner to call up your menu of options.

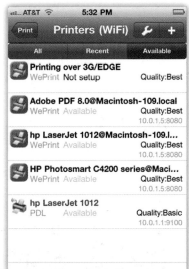

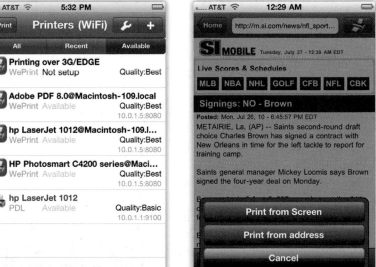

Best App for Saving Money on Calls

Skype

Free
Version 2.0.1 | Skype Software S.a.r.l
For all iPhones and the iPod Touch

By using the Internet's wiring instead of the cords and cables the telephone company uses, Skype lets you make cheap—and even free—calls around the world. Skype calls don't nick minutes from your phone plan, and iPod Touchers can get in on the action with a headset microphone. With the iOS4 update that brings multitasking to iDevices, you can now leave Skype running in the background to pick up incoming calls.

CALL SHEET: Skype works just like an instant messenger program: you add your friends and family's Skype account names to your Skype contacts list. When you see a pal pop up online, tap his name to call him. If both of you are using Skype, the call is free. If one of you is using a regular phone, you can still make the call but you need to pay a small fee (see next caption).

CREDIT CHECK: To call regular telephone numbers, you need to buy some Skype Credit. If you've never done so—or if you've burned up your last batch already—tap the My Info button. On the Info page, tap Skype Credit to bounce out to the Skype site, where you can exchange your credit-card number for Skype credits. Rates vary, but 2.1 cents a minute is the going rate.

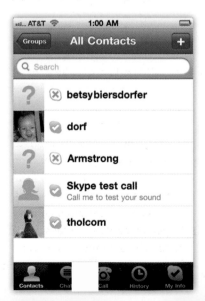

For Work

LONDON CALLING: Skype offers several plans and services, like your own Skype phone number for non-Skypers to call, as well as comparatively low rate plans for international calls. For example, for $13 a month on Skype's Unlimited World plan, you can call phone numbers in 40 countries. The various plans and Skype features are listed at *www.skype.com*.

Line2

Free | $14.95 monthly for full version
Version 2.4.1 | Toktumi Inc.
For all iPhones and the iPod Touch

Like Skype, Line2 uses Voice-over-IP (VoIP) technology to make phone calls over an Internet connection. True to its name, the app adds a second phone number to your iPhone, and you can make calls over Wi-Fi or a 3G data connection with it. With Wi-Fi, you don't even need an AT&T signal to call people. The app includes 20-person conference calls, visual voicemail, and more. It's free at first, but after 30 days, it'll cost you $14.95 a month.

TWO RINGIE-DINGIES: When you first start up Line2, you can pick an extra phone number in whatever area code you wish to use with the service. The same number works over a Wi-Fi or cellular connection to make and take calls. If you're in a weak area of cell coverage (imagine that) but have Wi-Fi access, you don't have to worry about missing the call.

Best App for Finding Business Numbers

Business Phone Numbers

Free | $1.99 for full version
Version 1.2.4 | Exact Magic Software
For all iPhones and the iPod Touch

Combining the Yellow Pages with local search, this app collects the digits of nearby businesses so you can reach out to the closest Best Buy and find out what time it closes or if they have the camera you want in stock. The app pinpoints your location and you can search for a business or store by name or keyword; doctors' and lawyers' offices are included. The free Lite version comes with ads.

DIRECTORY LOOKUP: Whether you're new in town or just can't remember when a favorite store opens, Business Phone Numbers can help. It first finds you by way of the iPhone or iPod Touch location services, so you just need to enter keywords or business names to find out what's nearby. When you type in a business name, the app charts its location on a map.

CALL OR GO: When you land on the map page, you see the address and location of the selected business—as well as your current distance from it. From this screen, you can tap the telephone icon to call the store's main number. To get driving directions from where you are, tap the road-sign icon to switch to Google Maps and a set of instructions.

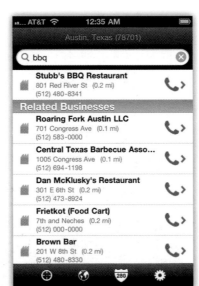

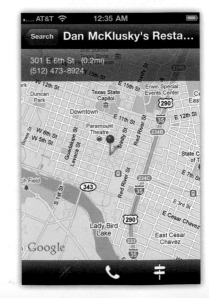

For Work

Best App for Hands-Free Calling

Vlingo

Free
Version 2.0.4 | Vlingo
For all iPhone 3G, 3GS, 4 and the iPod Touch

If you call clients all day long and want relief from constant tapping, Vlingo provides spoken-word dialing, as in "Call Tom at work." You have to make one initial tap to kick things off, but then there's no need to drill down in your address book or fumble with your Favorites list. True, the past few iPhone models come with Voice-Control for audio dialing, but Vlingo can handle web searches, Facebook updates, and map quests by voice, too.

AUTOMATIC FOR THE PEOPLE: Most people have multiple phone numbers these days, so when you tell Vlingo who to call, you also need to tell it *where* to call. The app waits a few seconds before dialing after it recognizes a name to give you time to back out. If you prefer to be the one doing the dialing, you can turn off the auto-dial feature in the app's settings.

VOICE COACH: Vlingo muscles in on Google Mobile's turf with spoken-word web searches for speedy surfing. Tap Maps here and recite a street address or a business name to see it plotted out. Vlingo also lets you update your Twitter and Facebook status. With a $7 in-app upgrade, you can add voice-driven email or SMS; $10 gets you both.

Best App for Finding More Apps

AppMiner

Free
Version 4.1.2 | Bitrino Inc.
For all iPhones and the iPod Touch

With the App Store surging past a quarter-million apps, finding what's new and interesting can be a little overwhelming. If that's the case for you, send in AppMiner. It has its own keyword search for finding stuff, but it's the Miner's ability to dig up apps on sale that makes it especially useful for bargain-hunters. If you really want to stay on top of it all, an in-app upgrade (for a buck) buys you push notifications of on-sale apps.

APP FOR APPS: To quickly see what new stuff AppMiner has dug up for you, tap the New button in the bottom-left corner of the screen. You'll see a list of categories that include newcomers. Tap a category name, like Business or Education, to see all the recently added apps in that area. You can filter the list to show only paid or free apps. Tap the ▼ icon to see apps released the day before.

INFO GRAPHIC: When you find an app that looks interesting, tap its name. Flick down the resulting Info page to see the developer's description of the app and a screenshot or two, along with the release date. Tap the Buzz button to run a Google search on the app or tap Share to tell a friend about it by email. Tap the Watch button to have AppMiner notify you when an app goes on sale.

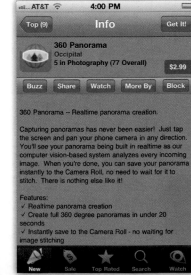

For Work

WANTED LIST: Once you add an app to your watch list, you can keep an eye on it in case you want to buy it later or the developer puts it on sale. (Holiday weekends are a popular time for apps to go on sale.) When you do decide to grab the app, tap its name to get to the Info page and then tap the Get It! button. This takes you to the App Store to seal the deal.

Appsaurus
$0.99
Version 1.5 | Hello, Chair Inc.
For all iPhones and the iPod Touch

Like AppMiner, Appsaurus is designed to help you wade through the ocean of code in the App Store, but it takes a more iTunes Genius/personal-shopping approach rather than just listing what's new. Appsaurus analyzes your tastes over time, based on what apps you look at and which you mark as favorites. Once it learns your preferences, it suggests other apps you may like. If Appsaurus keeps recommending an app you don't like, you can block the app.

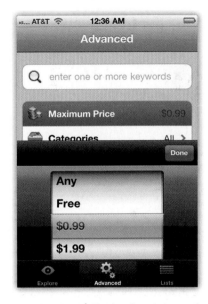

MAKING RULES: The App Store is vast and you may not care about hugely expensive programs or, say, business apps. If you want to give Appsaurus some guidance on what to find, tap the Advanced button. On this screen, you can enter keywords for the kind of apps you want to see, set up guidelines for the maximum price you'll pay, and pick the categories you're interested in. (Holiday weekends are a popular time for apps to go on sale.)

Best App for Desktop Remote Control

Jump Desktop

$19.99
Version 3.0.1 | Phase Five Systems
For all iPhones and the iPod Touch

The squint factor may be up there in James Dean territory, but if you need to remotely control your main computer over the Internet, Jump Desktop gives you the power to do so. The app, which supports both the RDP and VNC remote protocols, gives you a few ways to configure your system, and it works with all versions of Windows. You can control your Mac, too, by configuring it according to the instructions in the support area at *jumpdesktop.com*.

JUMP IN: Enter your desktop computer's IP address or hostname in Jump Desktop's settings to connect to your PC. You can also configure the app by installing a small bit of desktop software from the company's site and using your Google account to manage the login process. Once configured, tap the computer name to connect to it. It's like making a phone call.

MICROCOMPUTING: Once you make the connection, you can control your remote machine in either portrait mode (below) or the more spacious landscape view. The app lets you take over the computer's mouse by dragging it around the screen with your finger, but you can also connect a Bluetooth keyboard to late-model iPhones and iPod Touches for easier control.

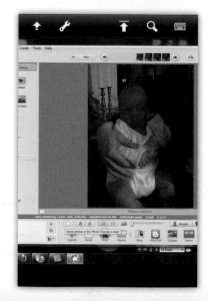

Best App for Password Storage

1Password

$9.99 | $14.99 for full version
Version 3.1.1 | Agile Web Solutions
For all iPhones and the iPod Touch

The need for strong, complex passwords has become increasingly important as more of your life moves online. 1Password turns your iPhone or Touch into an encrypted archive for not only your website and account passwords, but for other sensitive info too, like driver's license and serial numbers. The Pro version requires iOS4 and includes more features, like an easy-switch mode to paste your name and passwords into Safari.

LOCK BOX: 1Password does more than remember your Amazon password or online banking credentials. Tap the Add button to set up a record of anything you want to keep quietly on file, like software serial numbers or personal notes you don't want the world to see. Once you set up 1Password, you'll need to remember your four-digit passcode to open the app.

WHAT'S IN YOUR WALLET?: If you're new to the one-stop shopping approach to password management, the app provides plenty of preset categories. For example, when you tap "Wallet" on the Add screen, 1Password provides entries for all kinds of cards you carry around, including your driver's license and membership numbers for frequent-flier programs.

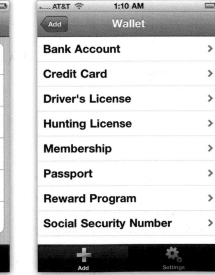

Best App for Monitoring Battery Time

Battery Magic
Free | $0.99 for full version
Version 4.4 | myNewApps Inc.
For all iPhones and the iPod Touch

Forget those numbers tossed out at Apple product announcements—how long does a battery *really* last? And how long does a charge last if, say, you want to play cell-draining 3D games? Battery Magic tells you (under two hours for the games). The Elite edition brings battery-care tips and a more detailed breakdown of how quickly specific apps will drain your juice. The freebie edition displays ads along with your basic power-cell stats.

APP-E-TITE: Start up Battery Magic and it immediately shows you a much more readable graphic of your battery status than the tiny icon on the iPhone or iPod home screen. While the free version lists the power consumption time of generic activities like "Audio Playback," the Elite edition pinpoints specific apps, like Pandora and AOL Messenger.

CELL DECORATION: Why settle for a boring old green battery when you can tart it up with argyle, a beach scene, or even a photo of the Golden Gate Bridge? Both versions of the app come with several stock colors, patterns, and images to dress up the power meter, and the Elite version lets you import your own photos. The changes, alas, don't show up on the home-screen icon.

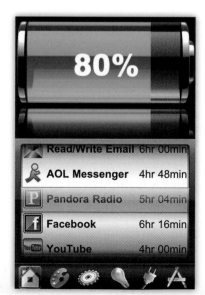

Best App for Updating Your Biz Blog

BlogBooster
Free | $4.99 for full version
Version 1.1 | 6taps
For all iPhones and the iPod Touch

Perhaps the biggest challenge to running a business blog is finding time to update it regularly so it doesn't turn into a dusty ghost site. This app, which works with most major blogware, lets you add text updates and photos while you're on the go—and lets you blog from places you normally wouldn't be able to drag a computer, like a movie theater. The free version has ads and only supports one blog at a time, but that may be all you need.

ACCOUNT ABILITY: BlogBooster works with all the big blogging programs and sites, including WordPress, TypePad, and Blogger. Just tap the one you use and punch in your user name and password to enable BlogBooster to add mobile updates to your site. You can also add a Picasa account into the mix and upload images from it to your blog.

BLOG THIS: Feel a post coming on? Tap open your blog account from the app's main screen and tap the Write New Post button. The next screen lets you title and tag the post and, once you start writing, a simple formatting bar appears above the keyboard so you can easily apply text styles. Tap the checkmark when you're done, then preview and publish the post.

Best Apps On the Town

If there's one thing the mobile Internet has done, it's foster spontaneity. No longer do you have to sit at home and browse the local newspaper for movie showtimes or museums you want to visit. With the right apps and a network connection—Wi-Fi or 3G—you can make your leisure-time plans while you're on the go.

Need to figure out the best vino to go with Cuban chicken or find the closest spot for dinner next to the concert hall? To **wine and dine**, you'll find plenty of apps in the store to help you, even when you're out and about.

In an unfamiliar part of town—or an unfamiliar town itself—but still want to find cool music and hot clubs? Many apps take advantage of the iPhone's GPS chip so they can quickly show you **what's happening nearby**. If going out on the town for you means just catching a movie, plenty of apps are dedicated to **the silver screen**; you can even rent a movie for your iPhone while you wait to get into the theater for another film. And dedicated **culture connoisseurs** can go beyond art-house films to find galleries, museums, book readings, and more with the right apps.

So, plans or no plans for the evening, make sure your iPhone's along for the ride. Odds are you won't get bored.

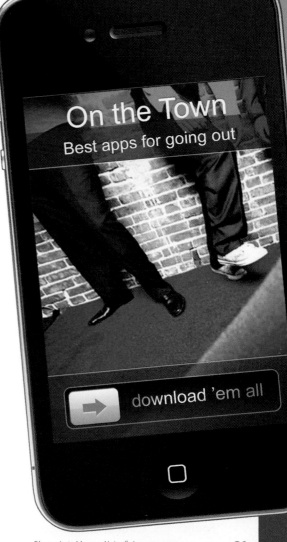

On the Town
Best apps for going out

download 'em all

Photo: Luis Munoz-Najar/luismuna.com

Best App for Previewing Menus

MenuPages
Free
Version 1.0 | New York Media LLC
For all iPhones and the iPod Touch

Many restaurants have websites, but who wants to dig around for one, especially if you're on the go? Menu-Pages lets you scour your town for a specific restaurant or cuisine and then shows you what's on the menu and how much it costs. The app covers eateries in New York, Los Angeles, San Francisco, Philadelphia, Boston, Chicago, Washington, D.C., and South Florida. Maps, reviews, and ratings make for a full-course menu app.

SEEK AND YE SHALL FIND: MenuPages finds and maps restaurants based on your location. If you've got a specific craving, search for types of foods ("salmon") in particular neighborhoods ("Midtown"). MenuPages displays the matches on a map. Tap through the list horizontally to see addresses, price ranges, and ratings.

ON THE BILL: Once you finish a first-level search, say for cuisine, MenuPages lets you refine your results. If you favor New American food, for example, you can further filter your results by restaurants whose dishes fall within a certain price range. Once you select a restaurant, tap "Menu" to see its fare.

Best App for Finding Local Restaurants

LocalEats
$0.99
Version 2.0.2 | Magellan Press Inc.
For all iPhones and the iPod Touch

Tired of chain restaurants? Fire up LocalEats to find one-of-a-kind chow houses in dozens of cities in the US and Canada. You can search by restaurant name, type of food, neighborhood, or feature. Alternatively, check out LocalEats' top 100 restaurants by city or its "Best of" picks for meal (say, best breakfast) or category (best diner). Choose "Nearby" if you have to eat *now*. In many cases, you can make reservations with a few taps.

GOING NATIVE: Whether you're scouting for a new place to eat in your home town or on the road in a strange city, LocalEats guides you to unique neighborhood hot spots from its database of 5,000 eateries. With an account on the app's website, you can add your own reviews and pictures to the mix.

HOMETOWN FAVORITES: Tap a restaurant name to find out which meals it serves (breakfast, lunch, or dinner), its price range, and its services (bar, parking, accessibility, and so on). You can also get directions to the place and see its location pinned to a map. Make a reservation with the tap of a key.

Best App for Pairing Wine and Food

Pair It!
Free | $4.99 for full version
Version 1.1 | Bandar Interactive
For all iPhones and the iPod Touch

Time-weary wine conventions, like drinking reds only with beef, limit your ability to discover new, inventive food-and-vino combinations. Pair It expands your horizons no matter what you're having for dinner. The app suggests 20,000 wine-and-meal pairings, and maintains details (description, flavor notes, pairing tips) on 180 wines. The app's free, ad-supported Lite version is less expansive than the full version.

SHAKE IT 'TIL YOU MAKE IT: Can't decide what to eat, let alone what wine to pair with your meal? Tap the Swirl button and shake your iPhone to let Pair It offer suggestions. Never heard of a dish? Tap its name to get more information. As a plus, Pair It gives you the recipe for many dishes right there in the app.

⊕ **HONORABLE MENTION**

iPairings
Free | $0.99 for full version
Version 2.0 | StoneRaven LLC
For all iPhones and the iPod Touch

Illustrated with big color photographs sure to get you thirsty, iPairings is a good app for beginners still puzzling over the difference between chardonnay and sauvignon blanc. It also delves into lesser-known varietals, like viognier and albariño. You can sort wines into reds and whites, and have the app pair food and cheese dishes with both flavors. The free Basic app offers 100 pairings, while the full version has more than 1,400 suggestions.

Best App for Choosing a Cheese

Fromage
$2.99
Version 3.1 | Steve Welch
For all iPhones and the iPod Touch

If your knowledge of cheese barely goes beyond Velveeta and you want to broaden your palate, Fromage is a worthy guide. This dairy database profiles more than 750 cheeses from France, Spain, Italy, the US, and Canada. It also offers impressively extensive wine-pairing lists. If you discover a cheese not in the app, snap a photo, type up a description, and email it to the developer for the next edition of the app.

SAY CHEESE: Fromage lets you search and sort cheeses several ways. You can find them by name, browse the cheeses of different countries, and sort by type of milk (cow, goat, and so on) or by the texture of the cheese (soft, semi-hard, and so on). Tap the + button to add an entry for newly discovered cheese to your Favorites list.

PAIR OR SHARE: Tap the name of a cheese to see suggested wine pairings. Tap the ☰ button for a fuller description of the chosen cheese. To add a cheese to your Try or Buy list, tap the Add Notes button, where you can also add comments or mark a cheese as a Favorite. Tap the Share button to email the cheese profile to friends.

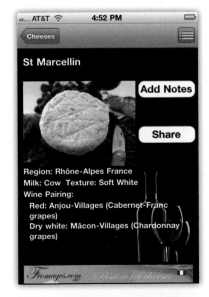

35

Best App for Figuring Out the Tip

CheckPlease Lite

Free
Version 4.3.1 | Catamount Software
For all iPhones and the iPod Touch

If you didn't pay much attention in grade-school math class, you may be stymied when it comes to divvying up the dinner bill and tip for a party of six. Luckily, CheckPlease Lite, a free, beautifully simple app, can help. Type in the total amount of the bill and dial in a tip percentage (which you can tell CheckPlease to round up, or not) or a dollar amount. Then enter the number of people sharing the tab and let technology do the math.

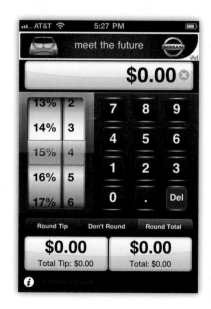

SPLIT THE BILL: CheckPlease Lite's clean design makes it easy to calculate your (and everyone else's) share of a dinner bill. You can specify how much of a gratuity you want to leave (a percentage of the tab or a hard number). The spinning dials make it easy to divide the check evenly, whether you have one or 100 dinner companions.

⊕ HONORABLE MENTION

Propina

Free
Version 2.1 | Paul Avery
For all iPhones and the iPod Touch

Utterly devoid of flashing graphics—as well as flashing ads—humble little Propina calculates bill divisions and tip amounts with a minimum of fuss. Just start up the app and type in the bill total. Tap the Next button and type in the percentage tip you want to leave. Hit the Next button again and type in how many people are splitting the bill. Propina then presents you with the amount each person should leave on the table.

On the Town

Best App for Mixing Cocktails

Mixologist
Free | $0.99 for full version
Version 2.0.2 | Digital Outcrop LLC
For all iPhones and the iPod Touch

Spanning the realm of cocktails from elegant pre-Prohibition classics like French 75 to the modern Peach Passion Jell-O shot, Mixologist brings a lot of boozy bang for your buck (or for free, if you don't mind ads). The app includes recipes for more than 7,900 concoctions, including non-alcoholic drinks. If you run low on ingredients, the app can locate nearby liquor stores or come up with drinks based on what you have on hand.

SHAKEN, NOT STIRRED: If you're in a rut of always mixing the same old cocktails, have Mixologist broaden your repertoire. Tap the Random button and give your iPhone or iPod Touch a shake. The app emits the soothing sound of ice tinkling in a glass and presents you with a randomly selected drink recipe. If you don't care for the suggestion, give it another shake.

⊕ **HONORABLE MENTION**

Pocket Cocktails
$0.99
Version 3.10 | Pocket Cocktails Inc.
For all iPhones and the iPod Touch

With a playful interface evoking the swinging '60s and huge color photographs of the featured drinks, Pocket Cocktails is bound to make you thirsty. The app includes hundreds of recipes, plus tips, tricks, and trivia for the home bartender. Tap Pocket Cocktails' Random button and shake the screen for a spontaneous drink suggestion. If you need a more informed selection to pair a wine with a meal, use the app's Pocket Sommelier.

Best App for Sharing Discoveries

Gowalla

Free
Version 2.2 | Alamofire Inc.
For all iPhones and the iPod Touch

Social networking has spawned the now-ingrained custom of sharing your everyday experiences with friends. A number of apps enhance the experience. Gowalla, like Foursquare on the opposite page, lets you find, visit, and share info about local spots, from ice-cream stands to funeral homes. When your network of friends does the same, you not only keep up with what they're doing, you discover new places to go.

TOUR MOBILE: Gowalla shows you the restaurants, nightspots, stores, and other points of interest around you, but it also offers unique suggestions, including specialized tours of certain cities that point out the cool things in town. You can "check into" each stop on the tour, collect a virtual passport stamp, and share your experience with friends.

GAME ON: While much of the activity on Gowalla involves discovering new places and sharing your adventures with others, the app has a game element that lets you collect virtual objects at certain locations and leave them for your Gowalla friends to find when they check in to the same place. You earn bonus awards by completing Gowalla tours.

Best App for Finding Your Friends

Foursquare

Free
Version 1.9.0 | Foursquare
For all iPhones and the iPod Touch

Foursquare, too, is a city-guide-meets-social-network app, but it emphasizes competition between you and every other Foursquare fan who leaves their home. Through the app, you "check in" to places you visit, see where your friends have checked in, and try to unlock special badges that show everyone just how social you are. You can even compete to be the "mayor" of a certain location—not by election, but by repeated visits.

FRIEND FINDER: So long as your friends use Foursquare and check into places as they arrive, you can quickly tell who's where. Tap the Nearby button to see which pals are geographically closest to you. You can see your Foursquare friends in list mode, or tap the globe icon to see them as dots on a Google map.

FLASH YOUR BADGES: Like the Boy Scouts, Foursquare encourages participation with rewards, in this case colorful little badges you collect to document your social accomplishments. If you want to extend your bragging rights, publish your check-ins and badge awards to your Facebook and Twitter pals.

Best App for Nightlife on the Go

NileGuide What's Next?

$2.99
Version 1.1 | NileGuide
For all iPhones and the iPod Touch

Covering hundreds of cities worldwide, NileGuide's What's Next presents a neatly organized list of your entertainment options in foreign lands and provides a handy button to add the most intriguing ones to your to-do list. In addition to nightlife, the app lists local hotels, restaurants, and touristy things to do. Built-in filters let you screen out the stuff you may not care about, like "boating."

EVENT PLANNING: Tap an icon at the top of What's Next's screen to see recommendations for restaurants, hotels, nightlife, and other activities. If you don't like scrolling through lists, tap the Map button to see the nightspots spread out geographically. As with most iPhone apps, you can tap the Near Me button to see the bars, clubs, and other places closest to you.

ON THE LIST: Some larger cities have so many things to do you need to pace yourself. As you find places to check out, tap the Add to List button to send items to the app's Quick List feature so you can find them easily. If you're new in town, tap the Snapshot icon to find articles on the area's history, local trivia, and seasonal weather patterns.

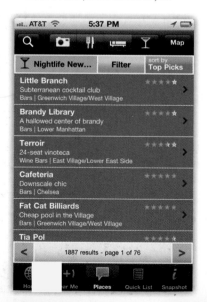

On the Town

Best App for Avoiding Parking Tickets

Parking Mate

Free
Version 1.0.2 | Tap Tapas LLC
For all iPhones and the iPod Touch

If you find yourself having nightmares about parking tickets, forgetting where you left your car, or marauding tow trucks, you probably live in an urban area with limited parking and lots of competition. And you would probably sleep a lot better with Parking Mate around. The app lets you set alerts so you can go feed the meter, jot down notes about street-parking schedules, and mark reliable spots on a map so you can find them again.

A METER FOR THE METER: Don't keep checking your watch and jiggling a handful of quarters during a meal, fretting over the time left on the parking meter. Set Parking Mate's timer before you leave the car. The app alerts you in plenty of time to stroll back and feed the meter. You can set the alert to go off from 5 minutes to 2 hours before the time expires.

LOCATION, LOCATION, LOCATION: Parking Mate lets you drop pins to mark the location of your favorite parking spots around town. Thanks to the iPhone's location services, you can tap the Drop Pin button to mark where you left the car if you've had to park in an unfamiliar area. If your spouse is using the car next, email the location information from the app.

Best Apps for Life's Little Necessities

ATM Locator
$1.99
Version 2.9 | Ombros Brands Inc.
For all iPhones and the iPod Touch

Unlike some ATM apps, which look for cash machines only in the United States or only for specific banks, ATM Locator lists about a million money dispensers around the world. The app covers bank machines, independent ATMs (the standalone ones that sprout up in delis and grocery stores), and the popular surcharge-free robot tellers that don't charge you $3 to take your own money out of your own checking or savings account.

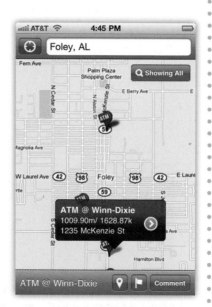

MONEY, THAT'S WHAT I WANT: If you're strapped for cash and in the middle of nowhere, tap ATM Locator's ◉ button to find the closest source of cash. You can also search by typing in the town name or ZIP code. Tap the Showing All button to filter your results to show just bank and independent ATMs. If you need written directions, tap the first icon in the bottom toolbar.

CoffeeSpot Pro
$1.99
Version 2.1 | CleverTwist Inc.
For all iPhones and the iPod Touch

For some people, coffee is a vital part of the day, from that first morning blast to a mid-afternoon pick-me-up. If you're on the road or away from your usual coffee shop, CoffeeSpot Pro comes to the rescue with a list of alternatives in the area. If you have a brand allegiance no matter where you are, set the app to show you only nearby Starbucks, Dunkin' Donuts, Peet's, Caribou Coffee, or other chains.

COFFEE BREAK: If you want a less predictable java experience, CoffeeSpot Pro seeks out independently owned caffeine emporiums. When you tap a shop's name, you get a detail screen. Tap the relevant icon to see where the shop is and get directions, call the store, mark it in your list of favorites, or even email a pal to join you there for a coffee break.

SitOrSquat

Free
Version 4.0.3 | Densebrain Inc.
For all iPhones and the iPod Touch

Desperate times call for truly helpful apps like SitOrSquat, which identifies and rates public rest rooms around the world based on its database and plenty of user contributions. Tap to see all the lavatory facilities around you marked on a map or in a tidy, organized list. You can filter the set of results to display just bathrooms that are currently open or facilities that include changing tables for the little ones.

RELIEF MAP: SitOrSquat lets you search for relief by neighborhood or current location, then draws up a list of potential potties. Tap an entry to get more info and see it on a map. The red, yellow, and green markers tell you if a loo is currently open; red means closed, yellow means the hours are unknown, and green means go—to the bathroom, quick!

Best App for Movie Mavens

Movies

Free
Version 4.0.1 | Flixster
For all iPhones and the iPod Touch

The App Store has dozens of movie mini-programs for finding current releases and reviews, buying tickets, and trivia quizzes, but if you want one that trumps them all, try Flixster's Movies. It offers local theater listings and showtimes, synopses, trailers, viewer reviews, and more. Film fans staying home for the night can also manage their Netflix queues and buy or rent movies from iTunes right from the app.

44

MOVIE NIGHT: Tap the Box Office button, and the Movies app shows you what's playing near you or in a neighborhood of your choosing. Each listing provides information like the MPAA rating, running time, reviews, and release date. Tap a title to view the trailer, find out where the film's playing, and add your own rating.

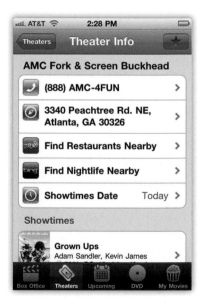

BEHIND THE SCENES: Going to the movies is just part of an evening out for many people. Once you pick a movie you want to see, use Movies' detail screen to see what you can do in the area before or after the show, courtesy of Yelp's neighborhood restaurant reviews and Bing's nightlife search listings.

TICKET MASTER: If the theater you're going to works with *movietickets.com*, you can buy your tickets right from the Movies app. Some theaters, however, work with a different online service, so if you don't see a Buy button here, you may want to download the Fandango and Moviefone apps as ticket-snagging alternatives.

EVERYONE'S A CRITIC: Thanks to its integration with *RottenTomatoes.com*, Movies compiles all the reviews from professional critics into an average rating. You can publish your own thoughts on the film by posting a review to Facebook from the app or by signing up for an account at *Flixster.com*.

HOLLYWOOD IN HAND: Tap a name in a movie's cast list to get a bio, photos, and filmography for that actor. The Movies app has other ways to help you kill time while you're waiting for the usher to remove the velvet rope, like taking movie-themed quizzes or browsing streaming video trailers of upcoming film and DVD releases.

Best App for Movies on the Go

Netflix

Free
Version 1.1.0 | Netflix Inc.
For all iPhones and the iPod Touch

Originally known for its little red DVD envelopes and speedy mail-order service, Netflix's movie rental business got even faster when the company introduced *streaming* video. With the official iPhone and iPod Touch app, you can browse and watch Netflix movies and TV shows wherever you can get a network signal. Although the service works either over a 3G or Wi-Fi link, go with the faster, cheaper Wi-Fi if you can.

MOVIES ON DEMAND: Sign up for an unlimited membership at Netflix.com (prices start at $9 a month), and you can instantly watch as many hours of online video as you want. The app displays new arrivals to the Netflix library and you can search for films by name or genre. This same plan lets you rent one DVD at a time the snail-mail way, too.

PUSH PLAY: Tap the Play button to start streaming your movie. Spin the iPhone or iPod Touch into landscape mode and grab some popcorn. You can fast-forward, rewind, and pause a movie at any time. When you pause a film on your iDevice, you can pick up the stream later—right where you left off—on a Netflix-enabled TV set or on the Netflix website.

On the Town

Best App for Going at the Movies

RunPee Mobile

Free
Version 2.0 | Rock Software Inc.
For all iPhones and the iPod Touch

You're not really *buying* that over-priced giant cup of soda at the concession stand so much as you're *renting* it. When nature calls on speed dial, this handy app tells you when you can duck out of a movie to go to the restroom without missing anything important on-screen (according to others who have seen the film). To avoid the wrath of your fellow audience members, check RunPee's cue sheet before the lights go down.

RUN TIMES: RunPee updates itself to keep its film list current. Tap a title to see where the breaks are in the movie's narrative action, their duration, and how far into the picture they occur. Want to know what you're missing? Bring your iPhone into the can with you—RunPee provides a brief plot summary of what happens during each break.

POTTY TIMER: If you don't want to fumble with your phone after the lights go down, set up a silent PeeTime vibrate-mode alert within the app. After you check the cue list and calculate how long your bladder can last, tap the timer icon in the upper-right corner. Tap the pencil icon to record the chosen cue time, then tap the clock icon to schedule an alert before the cue.

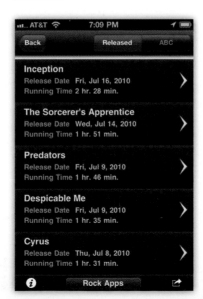

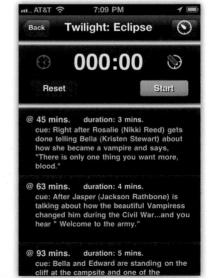

Best App for Locating Museums

Mused

$2.99
Version 1.1 | WeLike LLC
For all iPhones and the iPod Touch

Depending on where you are, you may be surrounded by museums and not even realize it. Mused reveals the educational opportunities around you, or in any other location you'd like to look up. The app points you to a variety of destinations, including art, history, and science museums and galleries, as well as larger installations, like the 301-acre re-creation of Colonial Williamsburg in southern Virginia.

GUIDED TOUR: Sure, you've heard of the Metropolitan Museum of Art in New York, but Mused covers both iconic museums and lesser-known collections, and tells you how to get there with help from the iPhone's Maps app. Despite its Mona Lisa logo, the original of which hangs in the Louvre in Paris, Mused currently covers attractions in the US only.

LOCAL BROWSING: If you want more information about a museum, tap its name in the search results, and then tap the View Website button on its Details screen. Instead of booting you into the Safari browser to complete your search, Mused takes you to a mini-version of the museum's website right in the app itself so you can quickly decide if it's worth a visit.

Best App for Finding Local Events

Goby

Free

Version 1.2.7 | Goby Technologies Inc.
For all iPhones and the iPod Touch

Goby does its darnedest to give you multiple answers to that age-old question, "Whaddya wanna do?" Its simple, three-button main screen gets right to the point, asking if you want to see "cool stuff today," make weekend plans, or see events in a different city. Choose one and Goby displays an impressively comprehensive list of local events in 350 categories (nightlife, family fun, outdoor recreation, and so on). So far, it covers the US only.

TO-DO LIST: Tap through Goby's menus to see more than 350 event categories, activities, and places to visit. Dog parks, wineries, casinos, spas, and recreational facilities are among the places the app keeps tabs on. If you're trying to keep the kids entertained, Goby has a whole section of youthful diversions, like water parks and bowling alleys.

RANK AND FILE: Goby sorts your results into a list, with numbered rankings based on your preference of relevance, date, distance, or name. Tap one of the buttons to resort the list to, say, find the events closest to you or that fall on a certain date. If you don't want to drive too far, tap the Filter button to change the distance radius of the events displayed.

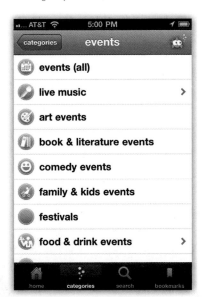

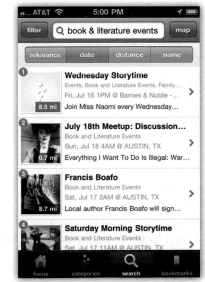

Best Apps For Leisure

As you saw in the first two chapters, you can find all kinds of apps for doing business or getting information when you're out and about. You might even get the impression that the App Store is full of no-nonsense tools that make you more efficient when you're on the go, but that have little to offer when it comes to downtime. That, fortunately, is not the case.

Extrovert or introvert, the App Store is loaded with programs that let you connect with the world or explore your artistic side. Into **social networks**? From Facebook to Bump, apps keep you linked into personal and professional communities in new ways.

When you're done socializing, you can spend some quiet time catching up on your reading. Whether your tastes run to **books and literature** or to fast-moving headlines from the world of **news, sports, and media**, apps can snag the latest best-seller right out of the air, bring you video of events happening halfway around the world, *and* show you the hockey scores.

You can also exercise your creativity. Apps that let you **rock out** and **make art** abound. Into images, moving or otherwise? Check out this chapter's suggestions to **enhance photos**, **make movies**, and **watch the tube**. There are even apps that let you **expand your mind**. Read on…at your leisure, of course.

Photo: Maerten Prins

Best App for Updating Your Profile

Facebook

Free
Version 3.2.2 | Facebook Inc.
For all iPhones and the iPod Touch

Five hundred million users strong and counting, Facebook dominates the social-networking scene. The company's own mobile app neatly shrinks the Facebook experience into a palm-sized dashboard so you can update your status and check in on friends when you're away from your desktop. The app doesn't perfectly replicate the website experience—among other things, some games may not work— but it's great for status-on-the-go.

CONDENSED 'BOOK: The home page of Facebook's mobile app collects all the popular parts of the site into one tiny screen. Tap News Feed to see what your friends are up to, or Inbox to read messages they've sent through the site. Tap the **+** button to create a page with shortcuts to your favorite friends' profiles.

PHOTO GALLERY: Facebook lets you manage photos on the go, too. Tap the photos icon to see all your Facebook photo albums and images. When you open an album, you see a page of thumbnails. Tap one to view the picture full-screen and to then flick through the album. Tap the **+** button to create a new album.

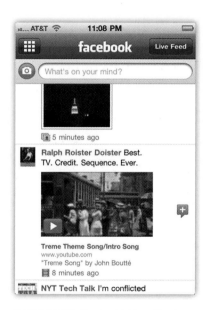

FEED READER: Facebook's News Feed feature lets you see status updates, photos, links, and videos of friends who have recently posted. You can post your own updates from this page by entering it in the "What's on your mind" box. Tap the camera icon to add a photo, either archived or freshly shot.

➕ **HONORABLE MENTION**

MySpace Mobile
Free
Version 1.7.2 | MySpace.com
For all iPhones and the iPod Touch

While outpaced by Facebook in terms of membership numbers, MySpace still boasts well over 100 million users. The site tends to attract more young people than its rival and has become something of a showplace for musicians to share sample tracks and keep fans up to date on tours and appearances. MySpace Mobile provides a streamlined window into the eponymous online network, letting you tap into friends' activities, blogs, and bulletins.

YOUR SPACE: MySpace Mobile's home screen puts your favorite MySpace social-networking features, including mail, photos, and friends, within easy reach. You can quickly update your status and mood—click the giant Update button—so your MySpace friends can follow your adventures.

Best App for Twitter

HootSuite
Free | $2.99 for full version
Version 1.1.5.3 | HootSuite Media Inc.
For all iPhones and the iPod Touch

Twitter is a way of life for some people, and a vital communication tool for others. Integrated with a companion website, HootSuite is a control panel for social-networking power users that lets you manage unlimited Twitter accounts, monitor and track replies and searches, and review statistics so you can see who clicks on your links. The free Lite version limits you to three Twitter accounts, lacks tracking, and includes ads.

GIVE A HOOT: HootSuite's Home Feed screen displays the current tweets in your account. Swipe your finger to the left to see your mentions in other Twitter feeds, direct messages, scheduled tweets for future posting, and sent tweets. Hoot-Suite also lets you update Facebook and MySpace profiles, WordPress blogs, Linked-In pages, and Foursquare check-ins.

HONORABLE MENTION

Twitterific for Twitter
Free | $4.99 for full version
Version 3.0.1 | The Iconfactory
For all iPhones and the iPod Touch

While HootSuite offers plenty of tweeting tools for Twitterholics, it might be overkill if you just want a nice, simple app for a single Twitter account. Twitterific for Twitter presents your feed in a soothing stream of gray, punctuated by white text and colorful profile photos. One tap takes you to a search box and a list of Twitter's current hot topics. The $5 in-app upgrade lets you ditch the ads and add multiple Twitter accounts.

For Leisure

Best App for Instant Messaging

Palringo

$0.99 | $4.99 for full version
Version 3.2.1 | Palringo Ltd.
For all iPhones and the iPod Touch

In the Olden Days of Instant Messaging, you used the service that most of your friends used and you didn't talk to people with the other instant-messaging programs. Palringo dispenses with that limited approach so you can send text, photos, and audio messages to pals on different instant-messaging networks. The paid version of the app lets you chat in landscape mode, see buddy icons, save IM messages, and pick different visual themes.

AT YOUR SERVICE: When you set up a Palringo account, you can add other instant messengers to it. The app supports popular services like Windows Live, AIM, Google Talk, Apple iChat, and even Facebook's own chat service. Once you add your user name and password for the services you use, you can log into them all through Palringo using just a single password.

TAKE A MESSAGE: When you start a message session with a buddy, the back-and-forth works just as it does on a PC or Mac. You don't have to run Palringo all the time to keep up, either. It offers built-in push notifications that ping you with a sound, on-screen alert, icon badge, or any combination of the three when you have new messages.

Best App for Emoting in Text

Emoji+
$0.99
Version 1.4.4 | Kolin Krewinkel
For all iPhones and the iPod Touch

In the early days of email, people turned to *emoticons*—punctuation marks arranged to mimic a happy face, a sad face, and so on—as short-cuts to telegraph their mood. Emoji updates that simple concept with more than 450 tiny, full-color illustrations that ride along with your iPhone text messages, Twitter posts, or IM chats. The Emoji icons show up only in apps that run on Apple iDevices, not in desktop mail or chat.

VISUAL LANGUAGE: After you download Emoji, you need to set up an Emoji keyboard via your iPhone or iPod Touch's Settings menu and Emoji's simple instructions. Once you do that, you'll see a newly added icon (⊕) next to the spacebar (below). Tap it to switch to Emoji's huge collection of pictographs, shown below right.

TALKING PICTURES: Emoji groups its images thematically (Travel, Plants & Animals, and the like). Tap a category and pick the icon (or icons) you want to insert into your message. Then tap ⊕ to switch back to the text keyboard. Once you write and emote, tap the Send button to share your thoughts and feelings.

For Leisure

Best App for Exchanging Contact Info

Bump
Free
Version 2.0.1 | Bump Technologies LLC
For all iPhones and the iPod Touch

Instead of typing up and emailing the same contact information to everyone you meet, try Bump. The app lets you exchange names, addresses, phone numbers, photos, and more simply by holding your iPhone or iPod Touch and knocking knuckles with another Bump user. If both of you run iOS4 (which works best on newer iPhones and iPod Touch models), you can also swap calendar events to help you coordinate your respective schedules.

FULL CONTACT: Bump works by using the iPhone or iPod's sensors to "feel" the bump. It sends the identities of each Bumper to its online servers and swaps the contact info (which you select). You can swap Facebook friend requests, LinkedIn details, and even Twitter feeds. If you update your contact info, you need to bump again.

PHOTO EXCHANGE: New parents can bump their baby pictures to friends and family instead of emailing 10MB of photos. The Bump app is also available for the Android operating system, which means iPhone owners can share information with folks using Droid phones or other devices that run Google's mobile-system software.

Best App for Reading Books

Kindle for iPhone

Free
Version 2.2 | Amazon.com
For all iPhones and the iPod Touch

With more than half a million books, including current best-sellers and periodicals, Amazon's Kindle Store is vast and varied. You don't need to buy an additional slab of hardware to use it either, as this Kindle app lets you buy, download, and read Amazon's eBooks right on your iPhone or iPod Touch. You can download a free sample of most books before you buy, and the store stocks an array of free public-domain titles.

ONLINE BROWSING: Tap the Get Books button (shown below right) to stroll through the Kindle Store. In addition to standard book categories like fiction and nonfiction, Amazon groups books by top sellers, new arrivals, and recommendations based on your past purchases. Tap a title that interests you to get more information, to try it, or to buy it.

BOOK STORE: The Kindle app's home screen displays the books or sample chapters you've downloaded from Amazon. Tap a title to open the book and start reading. The Archived Items area stores Kindle books you've bought on other devices, like an iPad or Amazon's own Kindle eReader. Since you already paid for the book, you can download the book again to read here, too.

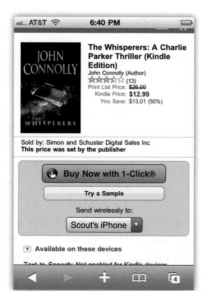

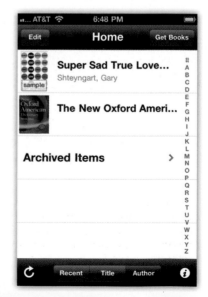

EASY READING: The Kindle app does its best to make reading on the small screen as comfortable as possible. Tap the **aA** icon to adjust a book's type size and color. Selecting the sepia background adds a brownish tint to the screen that can be gentler on your eyes. The app also has a built-in dictionary—just tap a word to see its definition.

iBooks

Free
Version 1.3 | Apple Inc.
For iPhone 3G, 3GS, 4 and iPod Touch 2G, 3G (requires iOS4)

From a design standpoint, Apple's elegant iBooks app is nicer-looking and more intuitive than Amazon's Kindle for iPhone app. It, too, has an integrated dictionary and the ability to search text. What it doesn't have is Amazon's massive inventory of books, which can limit your options if you want a book that hasn't turned up in the iBookstore. Still, Apple has thousands of new titles, best sellers, and plenty of free books to snag. You can also save and open PDF files on your iBookshelf.

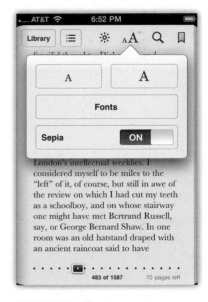

EYE BOOK: The iBooks app settings offer a choice of fonts, type sizes, and backgrounds (white or sepia). Buttons at the top edge of the screen take you back to your book collection or to the current book's table of contents. You can adjust the screen brightness, search the text of a book, or mark your place by tapping the bookmark icon.

Best App for Finding Nearby Books

Book Bazaar

Free
Version 1.9 | BayView Labs
For all iPhones and the iPod Touch

Reading books on an LCD screen isn't for everybody. If you prefer reading on good old treeware, your iPhone or iPod Touch can show you where to find the closest hard copy of a book. Type in a title, author, or keyword, and Book Bazaar retrieves your location and finds nearby bookstores that have your book in stock. If you're not in a hurry to get the book, the app displays prices from (and links to) online bookstores as well.

SEEK AND FIND: Type in keywords or the name of a book or author on the initial search screen and Book Bazaar looks around for copies of the book near you. If you're in an area with a lot of chain bookstores, you can see all its locations and check to see if the title is in stock not only at the closest store, but at other locations around town.

LIBRARY CARD: If you prefer to borrow rather than buy books, Book Bazaar checks local libraries for your title, too. Even if you're not searching for a book, you can use the app to find places to browse the shelves in person. Just tap the Browse button to see a list of bookstores and libraries near you or within a specified ZIP code.

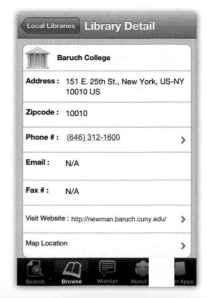

Best App for Perusing the Classics

3D Bookshelf Classic Literature

Free | $0.99 for full version
Version 1.0.8 | Ideal Binary Ltd.
For all iPhones and the iPod Touch

Stocked with about 40 historically popular literary works, 3D Bookshelf makes the most of its relatively tiny inventory by making the books look spectacular on your iPhone or iPod Touch. It presents its library beautifully, and "turns" pages in animated 3D detail, complete with a rustling sound. The app's free version gets you two titles: *The Merry Adventures of Robin Hood* and *Young Robin Hood*.

COVER FLOW: Much as you can flip through album covers on an iPod, 3D Bookshelf lets you browse its collection as book covers floating across your screen. When you want to read a title, tap the book and it opens majestically as the rest of the bookshelf fades to black.

DIGITAL PAPER: The text on 3D Bookshelf's animated pages echoes the classic typography used in letterpress book printing. Tap the wrench icon (shown below left) to invert the text and background colors (for high-contrast pages), and to adjust the brightness of the text and background.

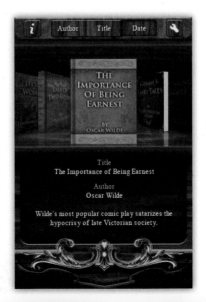

Best App for Following Superheroes

For Leisure

DC Comics
Free
Version 1.0.2 | DC Comics
For all iPhones and the iPod Touch

Superman, Batman, Wonder Woman, Green Lantern, The Flash—some of the best-known superheroes have come out of DC Comics, and the company's official app brings many of its champions to the touchscreen. While the app and some samples are free, downloads of recent and classic issues average around $1.99. It's a brand-new way to read comics—and you don't have to worry about ink stains or wavering piles of past issues.

MODERN ART: The DC Comics app gives you the option to see a whole page as it originally appeared in print, or to use a "guided view" that takes you from panel to panel, complete with animated transitions. You can adjust the time between transitions and even have the app automatically rotate wide panels into landscape view.

Marvel Comics
Free
Version 1.0 | Marvel Entertainment
For all iPhones and the iPod Touch

If Spider-Man, the Hulk, Iron Man, and the X-Men are your preferred comic-book heroes, feel free to mentally switch this app to the left side of this page. Both apps are powered by ComiXology's comic-presentation technology, so the main difference between them is the cast of characters saving the world. If you have no publisher allegiance and want an app that brings in books from DC, Marvel, and others, try ComiXology's own excellent Comics app.

Best App for Word Reference

Appzilla Reference

Free
Version 1.1 | Fossil Software LLC
For all iPhones and the iPod Touch

Taking up considerably less space than printed word references, Appzilla Reference is handy for quickly looking up word definitions—and more. In addition to a standard dictionary, the app includes a thesaurus and a reverse-lookup dictionary that lets you find a word by typing in a descriptive phrase. Appzilla also includes a spell-checker and a rhyming dictionary (for when you write your next song or poem).

BOOK ONLINE: Although Appzilla clutters its opening screen with an extremely large ad for one of the company's other programs, you can easily find the icons for each of its five reference books. Appzilla's content lives online, so you need a live Internet connection to look things up.

SOURCE MATERIAL: When you type in a word you want to look up, Appzilla rounds up a collection of definitions, including some with links to academic resources. The app also cites relevant entries on Wikipedia, the free online encyclopedia that anyone can edit.

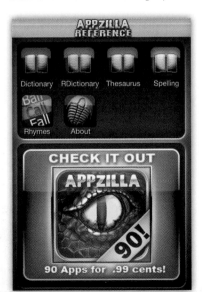

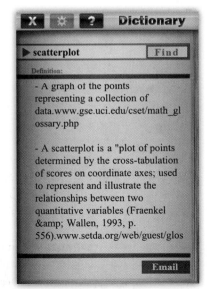

Best App for International News

BBC News

Free
Version 1.4.1 | BBC Worldwide Ltd.
For all iPhones and the iPod Touch

The news-gathering resources of the British Broadcasting Corporation are vast and wide—global, in fact. The Beeb's official app consolidates the day's big stories into a tidy grid. Tap a story square to move beyond the headline and get the full story. The app includes one-minute audio summaries of the day's news as well. True to its international reach, you can read BBC news stories in Spanish, Arabic, and other languages.

FRONT PAGE: The main screen of the BBC News app gives you a snapshot of current events. You can personalize the order of topics by tapping the Edit button and rearranging the news categories. Tap the Live Radio button to hear an audio stream of the BBC World Service channel as you browse stories on the home screen.

TV NEWS: In addition to text, many BBC News stories include a brief video you can stream in horizontal or portrait mode. To share stories by email or on Facebook and Twitter, tap the Share icon in the bottom-left of the screen. When you finish with a story, swipe your finger across the screen to move on to the next one.

For Leisure

Best App for National News

NPR News

Free
Version 2.2 | NPR
For all iPhones and the iPod Touch

National Public Radio covers the United States in depth over the airwaves, and its app brings the same stories to your iPhone or iPod Touch. NPR News sorts stories into topics like Business, Science, Books, and Technology for easy browsing. (It also offers world news.) Tap on a story's photos to see an article in full-screen view. Share buttons for each story make it a snap to spread the word by email or social networks.

AUDIO FILE: Tap your story choice on the main screen to see the top articles of the day or to ingest news by topic. Headlines that have the ◀)) icon include the audio versions of the story as NPR broadcast it. A button on each audio article lets you add it to a playlist so you can listen to it later. Tap the Playlist icon at the bottom of the screen to hear your selections.

ON THE RADIO: NPR is known for its regular programs on news, culture, and other topics. Tap the Newscast button on the main screen to hear that news stream through your speaker or headphones. If you want to hear the latest installment of NPR standards like *All Things Considered*, *Car Talk*, or *Weekend Edition*, tap the Programs icon.

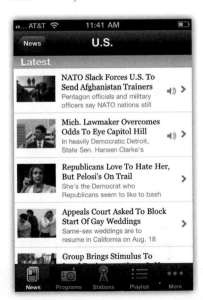

Best App for Local News

Local News, Weather, and More

Free
Version 1.2.1 | LSN Inc.
For all iPhones and the iPod Touch

Keeping up with world and national dispatches is one thing, but what about news that affects you personally, like events in your own back yard? Local News tries to fill the gap by rounding up news from more than 220 organizations (like TV affiliates) that cover local markets. Pick your location and browse news sources for your area. Some coverage includes school closings and traffic reports.

NEWS YOU CAN USE: Local News's info sources include local television stations and community websites, each bringing a tight regional focus to the news, much as a small-town newspaper would. And like a town paper, the app offers the local weather forecast, movie times at nearby theaters, and scores for local sports teams. Tap the More button to get lottery results.

MORE ON THAT: Tap a headline to get to the full story. Options at the bottom of the screen vary depending on the news source you tap into. Tap the button in the bottom-left corner to share an article with friends. Other news resources include video clips and photo slideshows. You can find daily horoscopes and a list of the cheapest gasoline prices with most sources, too.

For Leisure

Best App for Sports News and Scores

ESPN ScoreCenter
Free
Version 1.5.4 | ESPN Inc.
For all iPhones and the iPod Touch

ESPN ScoreCenter, from the sports-specific television network, lets you track the progress of your favorite teams in just about any major league. In addition to popular North American pro sports like football, basketball, baseball, hockey, and NASCAR racing, you can check scores from international favorites like tennis, soccer, cricket, Formula 1 racing, and rugby. Scores from the NCAA keep you current on the college scene, too.

TEAM SPIRIT: Tap ESPN ScoreCenter's **+** button to add a favorite team to your personal scorecard. Tap the bell icon to add push notifications for when a game starts, when someone scores, and final scores. Flick the screen sideways to page through scores from different leagues. Tap a score to see game highlights, or tap the scrolling headline at the bottom to get the full story.

Sportacular
Free | $1.99 for full version
Version 1.9.1 | Citizen Sports Inc.
For all iPhones and the iPod Touch

Sportacular is also an excellent app for keeping up with your teams as they grind through a season. Although its interface isn't quite as polished as ESPN's, Sportacular has nice features of its own, like a button that shows you pre-game odds and a one-tap view of a league's standings. Push notifications for game reminders and scores keep you in the loop all day. The paid Pro version liberates your screen from the clutter of banner ads.

Best App for Business News

Thomson Reuters News Pro

Free
Version 1.5 | Thomson Reuters
For all iPhones and the iPod Touch

Market news and financial information is vital to many Wall Street–related jobs, especially when the world's economy is so volatile. This app, from the Thomson Reuters news organization, gives you the latest corporate and financial news in one multimedia package. It covers the major market indices and the events that drive prices up or down, and lets you set up a watch list for stocks and companies.

NEWS BUSINESS: Thomson Reuters' News Pro app may have a business bent to it, but the outfit is a global news company in its own right. It rounds out financial coverage with other news of the day, including the latest sports and entertainment stories. Just flick down the News screen to see more categories, including the quirky "Oddly Enough" stories of the day.

LOUDER THAN WORDS: News Pro has plenty of visual bells and whistles, including a section of daily photos and video clips from around the world. To browse the photo collection, tap the Pictures icon on the main screen. Most clips in the app's Videos area are short—about one or two minutes—and you can play them in either portrait or landscape mode.

For Leisure

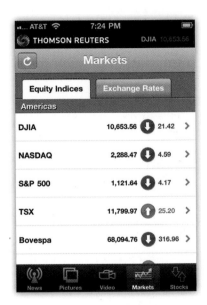

MONEY MARKET: Tap the Markets icon on the main screen to get a look at the state of the major financial indices around the world. You can also check the dollar's strength against other currencies by tapping the Exchange Rates tab. Tap the Stocks icon in the bottom corner to see current share prices, news, and company background information.

Bloomberg

Free
Version 2.10.3 | Bloomberg LP
For all iPhones and the iPod Touch

This app, from the Bloomberg financial news empire, is packed with market information. While it doesn't include videos, it does have a number of audio reports from Bloomberg Radio that add another dimension to the day's financial headlines. Bloomberg's default white and orange text on a black background may be hard for some people to read, but the color scheme works well when you flick through the long list of flag-tagged world markets.

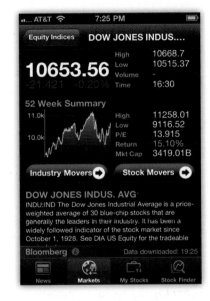

PRICE CHECK: To get the details on a major equity index like the Dow Jones Industrials, tap its name. Tap the Industry Movers button to see what sectors are hot, or tap the Stock Movers button to see the stocks that are leading—or lagging—the market. Along with equity indices, the app's Markets section lets you review bonds, currencies, commodities, and more.

Best App for Reading Web News

Reeder
$2.99
Version 2.1 | Silvio Rizzi
For all iPhones and the iPod Touch

This app gussies up Google RSS feeds (headlines and story summaries from around the Web) to keep you in the news loop *and* bring order and flexibility to your feed list. Reeder collects Google Reader feeds and organizes them by source, read versus unread, and so on. You can browse feeds individually or by feed folders you create, and share stories on Facebook and Twitter. You can also save articles that a feed links to for offline reading.

FEED THE MIND: Reeder complements your Google Reader feed and makes it ultra-easy to browse. It quickly reveals the number of unread stories you have in each of your feeds. To browse the headlines from a feed, tap the feed's name in the list to see the collected stories. Through Google, you can also subscribe to podcast feeds and stream the shows from Reeder.

QUICK READ: When a headline catches your eye, tap it to grab a short summary of the story. If you want the full article, tap the headline box to jump to the website that posted it. Icons at the bottom of the screen let you mark items as unread for later reading, bookmark your favorite stories, advance quickly up or down a feed, and share an item.

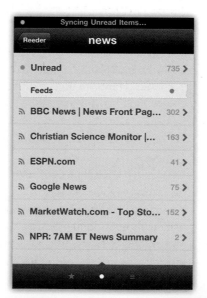

For Leisure

Info Junkie

$0.99

Version 2.2 | iPhone EZ Apps

For all iPhones and the iPod Touch

Not as lightweight or as streamlined as a regular RSS feed reader, Info Junkie still manages to unite 75 major mobile sites into one heck of a dashboard for serious newshounds. The sites range from major mainstream news outlets like the Associated Press and USA Today to cutting-edge tech blogs like Gizmodo and Engadget. Info Junkie isn't without its lighter topics, either—big network TV sports sites are here, as well as links to fluffy gossip rags.

SAVE AND SHARE: Reeder has shortcuts to several services that let you save a story for later reading on a site like Instapaper (turn the page for more on Instapaper's own mobile app). You can also share the story on sites like Delicious and Twitter. If you want to stick to time-honored methods of sharing, you can email the article or a link to it.

SIDE SWIPE: Info Junkie uses a horizontal navigation scheme to wedge in links to all the news sources it offers. Start by tapping a news category from the icons at the bottom of the screen. Then flick through the row of logos for websites Info Junkie includes in that group. Tap the name of the news site you want to read. You can add and delete your own sites, too.

71

Best App for Reading Web Pages Offline

Instapaper

Free | $4.99 for full version
Version 2.2.5 | Marco Arment
For all iPhones and the iPod Touch

Think of Instapaper as a sort of DVR for web articles. If you can't look at a story now, save it to your device with Instapaper and time-shift your reading to a later hour. You don't need to be online to read your saved stories. The paid version of the app includes goodies like folder organization, a dictionary, and adjustable fonts. And, like a DVR, Instapaper helps you skip commercials by peeling off the ads cluttering up the text.

PREPARE TO SAVE: For Instapaper to work its page-saving magic, you need to sign up for an account and install a special bookmark in your mobile Safari app. Later, when you're surfing Safari and want to snap up a story to read later, tap the icon and choose the special Instapaper: Read Later bookmark to save a copy of the text to your iPhone or iPod Touch.

DOWN TIME: When the day winds down and you finally have time to read all the stories you saved during your online travels, pop open the Instapaper app to see what's waiting for you (the free version of the app puts an advertisement on the main screen). Tap a headline to open an article. The saved story appears in comfortably sized type, ready to be consumed.

72

Best App for Public Service Channels

5-0 Radio Police Scanner

Free | $1.99 for full version
Version 16.0 | Dr. James Leung
For all iPhones and the iPod Touch

Breaking local news doesn't have to come from a mainstream media outlet—sometimes you can instantly find out what's going on by listening to municipal radio channels. 5-0 Radio Police Scanner streams these feeds—police, fire, public safety, train, plane, marine, emergency, and ham radio—into your 'Phone or 'Pod to keep you informed. The free version offers fewer feeds than the paid app.

RADIO HEAD: When you first start up 5-0 Radio Police Scanner, you get a menu that includes all the available scanner feeds and a Top 100 list of popular feeds (usually dominated by police departments in urban areas). From this screen, you can add feeds of your own using links supplied within the app. 5-0 Radio even has a bunch of music radio streams for your listening pleasure.

ONE ADAM 12, ONE ADAM 12: 5-0 Radio includes social tools for scanner and ham radio enthusiasts, like the ability to chat with a buddy over a Twitter feed while you listen to a radio stream. To decipher all the arcane emergency codes you're going to hear, the app thoughtfully includes a reference list of ciphers the police and military use.

Best App for Internet Radio

Pandora Radio
Free
Version 3.1.2 | Pandora Media Inc.
For all iPhones and the iPod Touch

Pandora grew out of the 10-year-old Music Genome Project, which analyzes songs down to their core elements of melody, harmony, lyrics, and other components. Using this info, Pandora creates playlists based on your favorite artists or genres. Name an artist and Pandora plays his and like-sounding music; give tracks a thumbs-up or -down to refine Pandora's tastes. An in-app upgrade ($36 a year) gets you the ad-free Pandora One service.

MUSIC PROGRAM: Start your playlist by naming your favorite artist. Pandora uses his or her songs as the foundation for its music stream. It relies on its song-analyzing algorithms to create playlists, and puts some very interesting tracks into the rotation.

74

⊕ HONORABLE MENTION

Last.fm
Free
Version 2.3.0 | Last.fm Ltd.
For all iPhones and the iPod Touch

This app may not buffer music as smoothly nor offer as many out-of-the-blue choices as Pandora's algorithms do, but Last.fm's huge library of 5 million tracks and rapt attention to your musical tastes make it a favorite of streaming-radio fans. Mark the bands it programs into your personalized rotation with the love 'em or hate 'em icons to guide the app. Last.fm has a ton of other features, too, like detailed band bios and listings for nearby concerts.

Best App for Traditional Radio

Radio

$0.99
Version 4.4 | Intersect World LLC
For all iPhones and the iPod Touch

Far cheaper than a shortwave radio, a mere buck streams 40,000 land-based radio stations through your iPhone or iPod Touch. The app includes the popular SHOUTcast directory of radio streams as well iTunes' list of Internet radio stations (so you aren't tied to your desk if you want to listen to web radio). You can tap into 2,000 European stations or stay closer to home with local public radio and National Weather Service broadcasts.

FLICK THE DIAL: The Radio app's list of directories lets you drill down through a huge selection of categories to find the type of music you want to hear. You can find stations that play only music from the 1940s, stations that play only music from film soundtracks, and every type of ethnic music out there. When you want a real eclectic mix, try college radio.

STREAM ON: If your device runs iOS4, you can keep listening as you move away from the app and on to other things, like surfing the Web or reading email. If you decide to hang around by the Radio app, the screen identifies the current station and the name of the current song and artist. Tap the Share button to get six options for sharing the stream or visiting the station's website.

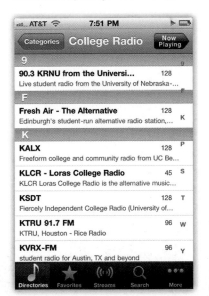

Best App for Streaming Your Music

Z-Subsonic
$4.99
Version 2.2 | Intulon LLC
For all iPhones and the iPod Touch

Hate it when your music library is too big to fit on your iPhone or Touch? Z-Subsonic streams your entire music collection from your desktop computer to your mobile device. It also plays audio formats that your gadget won't, like Ogg and FLAC files. Z-Subsonic communicates with a shareware program you install on your PC or Mac (*www.subsonic.org*), which turns your desktop PC into a music server and manages the streaming process.

MUSIC NETWORK: Even though Z-Subsonic streams music from your desktop computer, the app displays current track info (song title, artist, and so on) and gives you total control over playback (to pause, rewind, or skip songs). Tap an album cover to see a larger version of the art, just as you would on the iPhone or iPod Touch's Now Playing screen. To help prevent skipping and stuttering, Z-Subsonic buffers the music stream.

NOW SERVING: Z-Subsonic's shareware program turns your desktop PC or Mac into a music server (a file-storage computer). Unless you work in the IT industry or know the nuances of configuring servers, getting the Z-Subsonic app to talk to the Z-Subsonic music server can take some fiddling. You need to point the app to your music, which is the URL of your desktop computer. If you get hung up, visit the forums at *z-subsonic.com* for help.

Best App for Belting Out a Tune

Glee: Singers Wanted
$0.99
Version 1.0.6 | Sonic Mule, Inc.
For all iPhones and the iPod Touch

The Fox TV show about a band of show-choir misfits at a rural Ohio high school is a breakout hit for the network, and this app lets you live out your secret musical-theater dreams. Using the included tunes, sing into the iPhone or iPod Touch's mic while the app sweetens your performance by making pitch corrections and adding harmony. It's sort of like karaoke with help from a digital studio.

SING, SING, SING: The Glee app includes three songs from the first season of the TV show: "Rehab," "Somebody to Love," and "You Keep Me Hanging On." Pick the one you want and record yourself singing it—the lyrics appear on-screen as the track plays. You can turn on the pitch and harmony controls here as well. When you finish, save your solo to review or share it.

WORLD MUSIC: As with any cult TV show, "Glee" fans (known as Gleeks) share their love of the show with each other. The app lets you upload your version of a song for other Gleeks around the world to hear— just as you can hear their warbling. By sharing, you unlock new tracks to download and sing. You can also link to a 10-minute video tutorial from within the app.

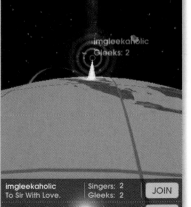

Best App for Learning Chords

GuitarToolkit
$5.99 | $9.99 for full version
Version 1.3.3 | Agile Partners Technologies LLC
For all iPhones and the iPod Touch

Guitar Toolkit contains a suite of utilities for the guitar and most other fretted instruments. The app includes a tuner, a metronome, and an illustrated library of half a million chords (and a button to adjust the chord positions for left-handed players). The cheaper Lite app has fewer chords and only lets you tune your guitar by ear (you don't get the more precise needle tuner). That works for microphone-free Touch owners, however.

FINE-TUNED: In spite of its name, Guitar-Toolkit demonstrates chords and tuning for just about any long-necked fretted instrument, like the four-, five-, and six-stringed bass guitar, the five-string banjo, the mandolin, and the ukulele. Along with the standard tuning for each instrument, the app has many of the common alternate tunings used for certain types of music.

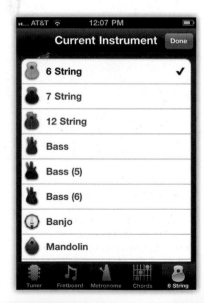

PITCH PERFECT: Once you select your instrument and the type of tuning you want, tap the Tuner icon to get those strings in shape. Pluck a string and watch the needle on the screen to see how sharp or flat the note is. Then adjust the string by tightening or loosening the tuning peg until the green tuner light indicates you've got a pitch-perfect note.

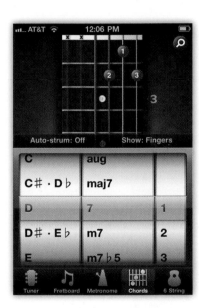

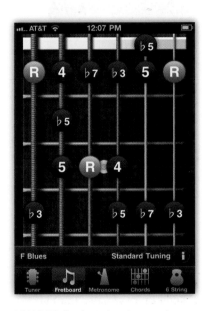

STRIKE A CHORD: When you need to see finger positions for a particular chord, tap the Chords icon and adjust the dials. The app illustrates the position of each finger on the fretboard. If you want to see the individual notes that make up a chord or the musical intervals (the difference in pitch between two notes) instead of finger positions, tap Show instead.

KEEP THE BEAT: Tempo is a critical part of a song, especially if you play rhythm or bass guitar and have to keep the rest of the band in time. Tap the Metronome button to get to the app's beat-keeper and use the horizontal dial to adjust the beats per minute. Tap the **i** button to change the counter's sound (bass and snare are options) or to pick a time signature, like 4/4.

SCALE UP: For those deep into music theory—or still learning it—GuitarToolkit is a great resource for understanding scales and the musical intervals of a chord up and down the fretboard. Tap the name of a chord on-screen to change to a different one, and then swipe your finger across the animated strings to hear the chord play at any fret position.

Best App for Getting Your Groove On

MegaSynth
$4.99
Version 1.2 | Mehmet I. Yonac
For all iPhones and the iPod Touch

MegaSynth proves that other keyboards can be even more fun than the one you use for typing. The app turns your iPhone or iPod Touch into a touchscreen synthesizer that lets you design and play your own groovy tunes. MegaSynth comes with more than 200 presets and you can spend hours playing around with them. You can save your compositions to the app or sync them over a Wi-Fi connection to your desktop computer.

STEP-SAVER: Mega-Synth includes a built-in step sequencer that lets you record and play back patterns of notes. The software can store 24 notes in a sequence. Tap the arrows on either side of the Tempo box to adjust the speed of the sequence.

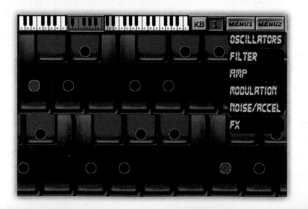

ON THE MENU: Tap the two buttons in the top-right corner to access the options for adding sonic goodies. Menu 1 offers special effects and oscillation, while Menu 2 includes presets, recording tools, and controls to make the on-screen keys bigger or smaller.

For Leisure

Best App for Requesting an Encore

Sonic Lighter
$0.99
Version 1.3.1 | Sonic Mule Inc.
For all iPhones and the iPod Touch

This app works just like a Zippo or traditional flint-based lighter—without the threat of setting your fingers on fire. To "light" your flame, strike the virtual flint with your finger. Once lit, you can blow on the flame (via the iPhone microphone) to see it dance on-screen or push it around with your finger to see it react. Turn the device sideways to see the digital flame lick the sides of the screen and start "smoking."

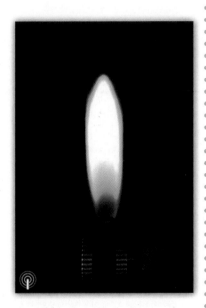

"FREEBIRD!": Much safer to wave around at a concert than an actual lighter, Sonic Lighter gives you options for flame size and color. Tap the antenna icon in the corner to bring up the app's icons. Tap the Settings icon to choose different theme colors (like Godzilla green [above] or King Kong yellow). Tap the globe icon to see where people around the world are using Sonic Lighter.

⊕ **HONORABLE MENTION**

iHandy Flashlight
Free | $0.99 for full version
Version 1.0.3 | iHandySoft Inc.
For all iPhones and the iPod Touch

This app has a series of on-screen lighters as well as virtual glow sticks for all your live concert needs. It also offers many other types of illumination, turning your iPhone or iPod Touch into a flashlight. When you open the app, shake your device to turn its screen into a bright white light for finding that elusive keyhole. The paid version has more than 60 types of lights to choose from; the free edition has fewer lighting choices and lots of ads.

Best App for Drawing and Painting

ArtStudio

$3.99
Version 2.9 | Lucky Clan
For all iPhones and the iPod Touch

More than a mere doodle program, ArtStudio is a full-blown digital illustration app that just happens to work on a fairly small part of a canvas. ArtStudio offers more than 30 drawing tools, including various pencils and brushes, to turn your finger movements into art that you can save and send by email—or upload to an online gallery. Happily, the electronic eraser tool doesn't leave little crumbs all over your creation.

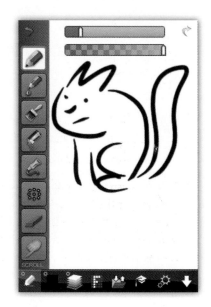

PALETTE CLEANSER: ArtStudio lets you work in different "media," including simulated pencil and a variety of paintbrushes. Settings let you control the thickness, transparency, and color of the lines. Want to change your brush settings or clear the screen and start over? Shake the iPhone or Touch to summon the Shake menu, which has five options for changing things up.

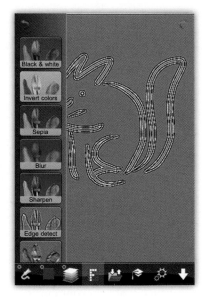

LAYERED APPROACH: After you finish the linework for a drawing, ArtStudio lets you add special effects to it to give your work a new look. Like desktop art programs, you can work in layers—up to five of them—to keep backgrounds and other elements of the illustration separate. You can blend layers together or rotate, scale, and move elements on a layer.

ART CLASS: With its collection of tools, ArtStudio invites you to start drawing. It also has an educational element for those interested in learning how to draw. To find the lessons, tap the mortarboard icon on the toolbar (shown on the previous page). Then follow along as the app automatically draws a line and invites you to trace over it to get the form and feel down.

Brushes
$4.99
Version 2.2.2 | Steve Sprang
For all iPhones and the iPod Touch

While it doesn't have quite the range of features or the built-in drawing lessons of ArtStudio, Brushes is an extremely powerful app for creating your own illustrations—so powerful that an image created with it was used on a cover of The *New Yorker* in 2009. Using the app's sensitive virtual paintbrushes, extensive color-picker tool, layers (which you can copy and paste between paintings), and ability to zoom in to 1,600 percent, you can create subtle and sophisticated artwork.

STROKE OF GENIUS: Brushes includes four sample images so you can get an idea of what it can do. Unlike oil or watercolor paintings, it's easy to correct mistakes after an errant brushstroke—an Undo button lets you remove a line with a tap. You can also import or snap multiple photos to create a collage, or to trace over a single photo to turn it into a "painting."

Best App for Virtual Sculpting

Phyzios Sculptor

Free | $4.99 for full version
Version 1.3.1 | Phyzios Inc.
For all iPhones and the iPod Touch

To add a new dimension to your art-work, try Phyzios Sculptor, a 3D carving program that lets you chip away at virtual blocks of wood by tapping the areas you want to remove. The block rotates on-screen so you can work from all angles. While the freebie edition of Phyzios Sculptor gives you just a virtual "chisel" to whittle with, the Pro version offers a wider range of carving tools, including a drill, a knife, and a file.

BLOCK PARTY: Before you start a sculpture, you need to pick the type of "wood" you want to use. Phyzios Sculptor gives you several grains and colors to choose from, and you can select the starting shape of your material, such as a box, a cube, a sphere, or a cylinder. If you want to sculpt on "softer" objects, you can carve art out of a virtual pumpkin or watermelon.

CHIP SHOT: The more you tap at a certain area of your "wood" block, the more material chips away, and you can start to shape the form you have in mind for your digital tree chunk. Drag the block to spin it on its axis so you can chisel away at other areas. The app lets you stop and save your work any time, so you don't have to finish your masterpiece in one session.

Best App for Temporary Brushwork

Zen Board
$0.99
Version 2.1 | Eight Bit Studios LLC
For all iPhones and the iPod Touch

Most art apps let you save your work and keep plugging away at it until you're satisfied with your efforts. Not Zen Board—true to Buddhist ideas about the impermanence of life, your brush strokes quickly "evaporate" on-screen, leaving you with a self-regenerating blank canvas to start all over again. The app is designed to be a soothing experience so you can let your fingers—and mind—wander for a while.

FADE AWAY: Zen Board's workspace resembles the spare simplicity of the Zen ideal, with just a couple of brushes and a water jar (so you can add ink washes to the canvas). Tap the ❶ button to adjust how quickly the "ink" disappears from the screen. You can also turn the effect off.

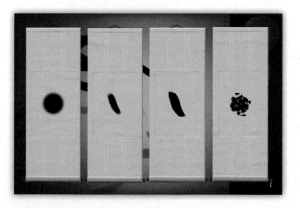

BRUSH OFF: Tap the two ink brushes on the main Zen Board screen to call up the app's brush picker. With four brush types to choose from, Zen Board is well suited to those who want to practice calligraphy strokes—and you never have to worry about stopping to erase your canvas.

85

Best App for Improving Your Photos

Adobe Photoshop Express
Free
Version 1.2.2 | Adobe Systems Inc.
For all iPhones and the iPod Touch

Adobe now offers a version of its powerful desktop image-editing program, Photoshop, as an app dedicated to improving your pictures. The app lets you crop photos, adjust contrast, and make other fixes. You can work on images from your device's synced photo library or on pics from the iPhone's Camera Roll. And when you sign up for a free account at Photoshop.com, you get 2GB of server space to store and display pics.

PRETTY AS A PICTURE: Photoshop Express obviously doesn't have the warehouse of features that the desktop version has, but it keeps the most common tools set intact. Tap a menu to reveal the controls for changing a picture's exposure, tint, contrast, and more. You can also crop, rotate, and add filters and effects to photos.

TOOL TIPS: If you've never used a photo-editing program, the learning curve can seem steep, but Photoshop Express guides you along. As with most helper programs, once you learn the software, you don't need boxes popping up in your face at every turn, so the app gives you the option to hide the tips.

For Leisure

Rectangle

Borders

SHOW-OFF: To physically frame your shot, the app gives you a choice of border types. Tap one to use it. When you're done editing your picture and want to show it off, you can upload it right from the app to Photoshop.com, your Facebook page, or to TwitPic. You can also save it to your photo library and email it.

PhotoForge
$2.99
Version 1.93 | GhostBird Software
For all iPhones and the iPod Touch

PhotoForge does many of the same things (and more) that Photoshop Express does, but it doesn't offer integrated online storage and it may take longer for newcomers to learn. Still, if you're familiar with the standard features of most image editors, you'll do fine. PhotoForge has all the tools you need to do pretty much anything to a pic, including crop and smudge it. The app also includes paint tools so you can create original artwork from a blank canvas.

PIXEL PERFECT: You name it, Photo-Forge can probably do it: crop, rotate, fill, smudge, or filter. The app lets you adjust just about every characteristic of a pic, including its curves, levels, hue, saturation, brightness, and contrast. If you don't feel like futzing around, the app can automatically adjust white balance and exposure.

Best App for Retro Photography

SwankoLab
$1.99
Version 1.0.1 | Synthetic Infatuation LLC
For all iPhones and the iPod Touch

The arrival of digital cameras made splashing around in a darkroom full of chemicals a thing of the past, which is a shame because many famous photos (like Ansel Adams's "Moonrise, Hernandez, New Mexico") were refined in the darkroom. For an inventive re-creation of those darkroom days, try SwankoLab. It gives you eight "chemicals" (photo-processing effects) to apply to pictures from your photo library.

CHEMISTRY SET: SwankoLab's playful interface mimics an actual darkroom, complete with several bottles of chemicals on the shelf above the developer tray. To get started, select a photo from your library, and then select the chemical (or chemicals) you want to use on it. The animated bottles actually apply different filters and visual effects to your photo.

DEVELOPING SITUATION: Once you add the right dashes and doses of effects to the mix, pull the on-screen lever to lower the selected photo into the developer tray. Through nimble animation, you see your picture drop into the tray and slowly "develop" as a photo timer ticks away. An on-screen notebook lets you store your favorite "chemical" combinations.

Hipstamatic

$1.99
Version 160 | Synthetic Infatuation LLC
For all iPhones and the iPod Touch 4G

In an apparent celebration of vintage photography, the company behind SwankoLab makes Hipstamatic, too. It turns your iPhone's camera into one of those cheap plastic 20th-century snapshot boxes—and makes the pictures you shoot with it look like authentic analog-era prints. You can change the look of the resulting images by swapping out the camera's virtual lenses, flashes, and film types. An in-app option lets you buy more downloadable gear.

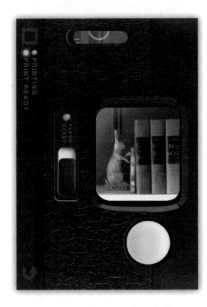

FINISHED PRINTS: Once you "process" your picture, SwankoLab clips it to a virtual clothesline to "dry." Tap the image to see it full-screen. From here, you can save the Swankofied picture to your photo library. The app's ability to combine effects, like the warm, oversaturated colors of art prints and the rich noir filter shown here, encourages plenty of experimentation.

SQUARE SHOT: When you launch Hipstamatic, your iPhone takes on the look of the original Hipstamatic toy camera that was around for about 5 seconds in 1982. Line up your shot in the viewfinder (which works in landscape or portrait mode) and press the big yellow shutter button to snap your pic. You can save HipstaPrints to your library or share them online.

Best App for Taking Better Photos

Camera One
$0.99
Version 3.5 | CocoaTek LLC
For all iPhones and the iPod Touch 4G

The iPhone's built-in camera got a lot better with the iPhone 4, but even with more megapixels, there's room for improvement. Camera One adds to the iPhone many features found in standard cameras, including a timer for self-portraits and optional timestamps printed right on your pics. A 4× digital zoom brings subjects closer, and you can convert color photos to moody black-and-white, or add a sepia tint to get an antique-photo effect.

EVEN KEEL: To help line up shots and eliminate crooked angles, Camera One overlays a grid on the screen so you can get things straightened out before you snap. If you find you shake the camera when you reach for the shutter button, take the picture using the app's cool voice command. All you have to do is line up the subject and say "cheese" to your iPhone.

ALL SHOOK UP: Like many digital cameras, Camera One includes a feature that automatically stabilizes your shots, which can cut down on blurry photos. The toolbar at the top of the screen holds the app's feature controls, like the shutter delay. Tap the *i* icon to get to the app's settings, where iPhone 4 owners can choose between the front and back camera.

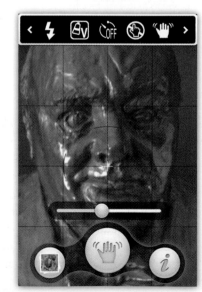

For Leisure

Best App for Underexposed Shots

Night Shot Deluxe
$0.99
Version 2.1.1 | Imaging Luminary LLC
For all iPhones and the iPod Touch

The iPhone 4 was the first model to come with an actual flash for its camera—but that doesn't help people using older models. If you find your images dark and murky (even ones you sync to an iPod Touch), this app may help. When you take a picture, Night Shot Deluxe gives you the option to brighten up photos the way a physical camera flash would—without you having to go out and buy a whole new iPhone.

LIGHT THE WAY: Despite the name, you can use Night Shot Deluxe any time you don't have enough light to brighten areas lost in shadows (or even to enhance shots taken when the iPhone 4 flash fired but wasn't bright enough). You can add light to a shot you're about to take, or dig up an old too-dark picture from your photo library.

FLASH MOB: Night Shot Deluxe offers several intensities of "flash." Tap the button for Flash, More Flash, and High Flash to see how a picture changes as the software mimics the effects of a real flash. Tap the Modes button to alter the look of a photo even more by converting it to black-and-white or the brown-tinged sepia tone seen in old prints.

Best App for Wide-Angle Shots

AutoStitch Panorama

$2.99
Version 3.0 | Cloudburst Research Inc.
For all iPhones and the iPod Touch

City skyline or majestic mountain view—every once in while you want to take a picture that's wider than your iPhone camera's frame. That's when software that combines several overlapping images into one big, Cinemascope-worthy photo comes in. As its name implies, AutoStitch Panorama electronically "stitches" together up to 30 images to fully capture a view.

A STITCH IN TIME: Several apps in the App Store create lovely panoramas, but many require that you shoot the images as the app "stitches" them together. Auto-Stitch Panorama lets you take the photos first, then personally select the shots you want to use for the panorama. This way, you can weed out dupes and duds. Touch users can use the app with imported pics.

THE BIG PICTURE: Once you select the photos you want to quilt together, tap the Stitch button. The app matches up overlapping parts of the pictures, lines up elements, and renders the panorama. When it's done, the app displays the stitched image on-screen. Next, slice off the uneven edges with the app's Crop tool. Finally, tap to save or share your view with friends.

Best App for Sharing Photos Online

Flickr Master

$0.99
Version 1.3 | Intersect World Inc.
For all iPhones and the iPod Touch

The Flickr photo-sharing site has its own mobile app, but this one lets you see and share your photography a little more directly. If you have an iPhone, you can snap a picture and upload it right to your Flickr page, simultaneously notifying your friends on Facebook, MySpace, and Twitter. You can also upload images from your photo library and see your Flickr photostream (all the pictures you've ever uploaded to the site) at a glance.

STRAIGHT SETS: Once you log into your Flickr account, you can see your pictures in several ways: grouped by albums (called "sets" on Flickr), by photostream, or by keywords you added to your photos. Tap the Contacts button to see what your Flickr friends have been shooting lately, or the Camera button to shoot and send a photo to Flickr right now.

REAL-TIME SHARING: With an Internet connection, you can browse all the images you stored on Flickr in full-screen view, just as you can when you look at photos from your iPhone or iPod Touch photo album. Tap the arrows at the bottom of the screen to cycle through the photostream or photo album as you show off your pics to friends in person.

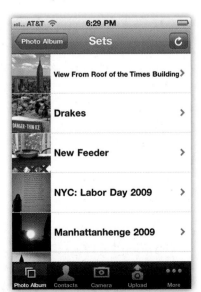

93

Best App for Making iPhone Movies

ReelDirector
$3.99
Version 3.2 | Nexvio Inc.
For all iPhones and the iPod Touch

If your iPhone can shoot video, why not have an app that lets you trim out the dull parts, add some Hollywood-style effects, and upload your own mobile mini-movie to YouTube? That's what ReelDirector does. The app works with all iDevices, but you have to copy and paste into the app clips you import on older iPhones and iPod Touches. If your device has iOS4, you can also import iPod music to use as your movie's soundtrack.

TIMELINE TALES: The ReelDirector app looks and acts like a shrunken-down desktop video-editing program. When you start a new project, tap the **+** button to import your videos, photos, iPod music, newly recorded sound, or clipboard contents into the editing timeline. Once there, you can drag-and-drop the clips into any order you want.

IN TRANSITION: Like any good editing program, ReelDirector lets you add animated transitions that gracefully move you from scene to scene. You can choose from 28 styles (cross-dissolves, fades, wipes, and so on). The app displays words over your moving pictures, too, so you can overlay text on your video to add titles and credits for a more professional look.

For Leisure

VERDICT RENDERED: Once you add all the video clips, photos, audio, music tracks, transitions, and titles to your project, it's time to mash it all together into a movie, a process called rendering. Once you render your movie—which can take a few minutes—you can export it for others to see, say on YouTube. You can also save movies to your Camera Roll or email them.

⊕ HONORABLE MENTION

iMovie
$4.99
Version 1.0.1 | Apple Inc.
For the iPhone 4 and iPod Touch 4G

Apple has had its own Mac video-editing software, iMovie, for years, and the company recently created a mobile version as an iPhone app. While it's well-designed and easy to learn (especially if you already know the desktop version), it works only on the iPhone 4 and the latest Touch, which leaves a lot of people out. But if you have the latest phone, you can create and edit movies wherever you are and upload them to YouTube or to your MobileMe gallery (if you subscribe to MobileMe).

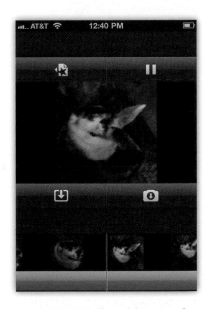

MOVIE PREVIEWS: The mobile version of iMovie offers the same timeline tools that you find in the desktop version, so you can edit, arrange, and preview your movie. You can use tunes from your library as a soundtrack, or use pre-stocked iMovie music. After you trim your clips and add transitions, you can export the finished movie in one of three resolutions: medium, large, or HD.

95

Best App for Creating Cartoons

Animation Creator
Free | $1.99 for full version
Version 1.7.2 | Red Software LLC
For all iPhones and the iPod Touch

As anybody who's ever seen an animated film knows, you don't need real people or places to make a movie. Animation Creator turns your iDevice into a pocket cartoon studio. Hand-drawing your action frame by frame isn't the fastest way to make a movie, but the app teaches you the principles of old-school animation, the kind the Disney studios used to do. The free Lite version allows only three projects with 15 frames of movement each.

FIRST FRAME: Whatever you can draw, you can animate with Animation Creator. Here, a standard-issue stickman makes a good first subject. The app includes a set of the basic brush tools found in most drawing programs. Tap the brush tool to open the palette (shown on the opposite page). Tap the dot next to the brush to change the line thickness.

IN MOTION: After you draw an initial object, tap the Duplicate button (it looks like two squares) to copy it, and then click the **+** button to add a new frame with the copied image. You need to change the position of some part of the figure to simulate motion. Here, the right leg is erased and redrawn at a new angle to make it "move." The gray line shows the original position.

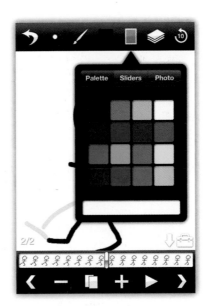

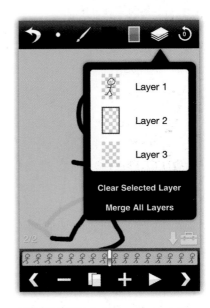

TOOL BOX: To summon Animation Creator's toolbar, tap the screen with three fingers. You can switch tools by tapping the brush or selected tool at the top of the screen. Your tools include an eraser to remove existing lines and to correct mistakes, and geometric shapes you can add to a frame. You can also import pictures from your photo library.

BEHIND THE ACTION: A plain white background is one way to go, but you can add color to your cartoon, or even have it play on top of a photo from your library. Tap a stock color in the Palette tab to add a background shade. If you want a custom color, tap the Sliders tab and adjust the red, green, and blue controls until you get the shade you want. Tap Photo to pick a pic.

FRESH LAYERS: As with most art- and photo-editing programs, you can use layers as you draw so you can work on different elements of a frame before you combine all the layers into a single frame. Layers are great when you have objects that need to move independently of each other, like two cars or two people passing by one another.

Best App for Video on Older iPhones

iCamcorder
Free | $1.99 for full version
Version 2.0 | Drahtwerk
For the iPhone 2G and 3G

Just because you haven't upgraded your first- or second-generation iPhone doesn't mean you can't add new features yourself. This app lets your older iPhone capture video at a rate of 15 frames per second and save the clip so you can email it or share it on popular social-networking sites. The paid version gives you unlimited recording time, but the free edition lets you capture only 15 seconds of footage at a time.

ROOM TO ZOOM: Shooting television-style video works best when you have plenty of light so you can see the action, and plenty of close-ups to make the shot interesting. iCamcorder offers a digital zoom of 2× or 4× so you can move in and out of a shot. To change the zoom level, tap the button in the lower-left corner.

SPECIAL EFFECTS: Like the retro-photography apps seen earlier in this chapter, iCamcorder lets you apply one of 11 effects to your video clips to make them look like they're from a certain era. You can also adjust the quality of the video (to get a smaller file size, for example), and film your clips in either landscape or portrait mode.

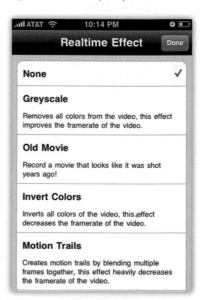

Best App for Streaming Video

Ustream
Live Broadcaster
Free
Version 1.4 | Ustream.tv Inc.
For iPhone 3G, 3GS, and 4, and the iPod Touch 4G

Combine this app with an Internet connection and you turn your iPhone into a live webcam, broadcasting whatever it's pointed at to a video feed on Ustream's website. It's great for those kids' soccer games when not everyone can be there or when you want to show off a new litter of puppies. The app can even send an automatic tweet and link to your Twitter followers when your live broadcast begins.

LIVE, FROM WHEREVER: To stream live video to the Web, you need to sign up for a free account at *Ustream.tv* so your broadcast has a home. Then you just need something to record, like a birdfeeder about to be mobbed by sparrows or a baby revving up to crawl. People watching your stream can type in chat comments or participate in live online polls.

PRE-RECORDED EARLIER: If you don't have a network connection at the moment, Live Broadcaster lets you record video straight to your iPhone. This also lets you preview recorded clips before you show them to other people on the Web. When you're ready, hit the Upload button to send the file to the Ustream site, or to Facebook, Twitter, or YouTube.

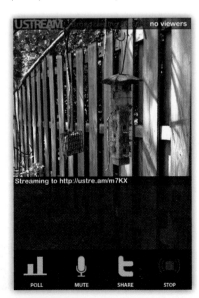

Best App for Planning Your TV Time

TV Guide Mobile
Free
Version 1.4.1 | Roundbox Inc.
For all iPhones and the iPod Touch

The national publication that started out in the 1950s as a pulpy little digest crammed with weekly television schedules and news has gotten even smaller—but much more interactive. The official TV Guide app zeroes in on your personal channel listings after you supply your ZIP code and cable provider so you can see the air date, scheduled time, and episode description of your favorite programs. You still get TV news, too.

LOG LINES: After you tell TV Guide Mobile where you live and what cable provider you use, it displays the TV lineup for your area. You can browse away and make notes of what you need to punch into your DVR. Tap the title of a show to see a description and more information (rating, network, and so on). The app also has a search function so you can track down specific programs.

PERSONAL PROGRAMMING: When you check out a show, tap the Add Favorite Channel or Add Favorite Program button to add it to your Favorites list. You can check the Favorites area to see upcoming shows only on channels you like or to check the schedule to see whether a much-loved program is airing a new episode or if it's a repeat.

Best App for Watching Vintage TV

Hulu Plus

Free | $10 monthly for full version
Version 1.0 | Hulu LLC
For all iPhones and the iPod Touch

The Hulu app itself is free, and *Hulu. com*'s Free Gallery gives you a taste of what you can watch. But to see the good stuff, you have to pay $10 a month for a Hulu Plus subscription. That monthly ten-spot brings much more to your handheld screen. You can choose from thousands of episodes of various shows, including current programs from ABC, Fox, and NBC; and entire series and seasons of old shows like *The X-Files* and *Buffy, the Vampire Slayer*.

VIDEO LIBRARY: Even without a subscription, you can browse Hulu to see what it offers to the devoted fans who do pay up. It lists shows by series, episode title, season, and episode number. When you get tired of seeing what's popular, you can search for favorite shows from the thousands of classics Hulu has on file. To subscribe, go to *hulu.com/plus*.

WATCH ME: Hulu Plus's Featured area shows all the programs Hulu currently highlights, including full movies, random episodes of network television shows, and even independent comedy shorts like the *Chad Vader: Day Shift Manager* series that got its start on the Internet. When you find a show you want to watch, you can view it in landscape or portrait mode.

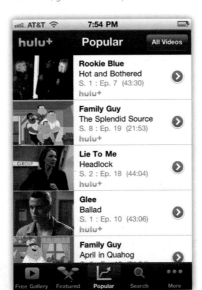

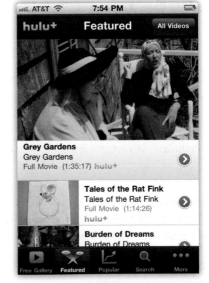

Best App for Watching Live TV

MobiTV
Free | $10 monthly for full version
Version 4.0.57 | MobiTV Inc.
For all iPhones and the iPod Touch

Like Hulu, this app gives you a taste of video for free but requires a subscription to watch popular TV channels. You can choose from several live channels, including ESPN Mobile, NBC Sports Mobile, MSNBC, and Fox News. On Demand offerings include shows from Comedy Central, Syfy, and more. Subscriptions start at $10 for one month, but you can pay $25 for three months or $45 for six months of full MobiTV service.

TV ON TAP: If you miss one of your favorite television shows, see if MobiTV has it on tap so you can watch it on your iPhone or iPod Touch. Tap the On Demand button at the top of the screen to browse MobiTV's shows.

GOING LIVE: The Live Channels lineup streams real-time TV to your handheld, making it a great way to sneak in a U.S. Open match on your lunch break or to keep up with breaking news. Tap the screen to make the playback controls go away.

Best App for Watching Live Baseball

MLB.com at Bat

Free | $14.99 for full version
Version 1.2.1 | MLBAM, L.P.
For all iPhones and the iPod Touch

Serious baseball fans need constant infusions of info, from Opening Day through the World Series. MLB.com at Bat lets you watch one live streaming game each day of the regular season. (If you have a $40 annual MLB.TV subscription, you can watch more live games.) Live television broadcasts aside, the app offers live audio of all the games, video highlights, and more box scores than you can shake a bat at.

TAKE ME OUT: Even if you're far away from the nearest TV or computer screen, you can keep up with the Boys of Summer. If you have the full MLB.TV subscription, you can watch live games on the go, although blackout restrictions do pop up at certain times.

BALLPARK FIGURE: It may be pricey, but MLB.com at Bat delivers a lot of bang for baseball fans' buck. In addition to video and audio game feeds, the app keeps you up to date with league news, current standings, and exclusive content for fans who happen to actually be at a game. The free Lite version gives you just scores, schedules, and standings.

Best App for a Meditative Mood

Zen Master Bundle

$1.99
Version 1.0 | Tesla Software LLC
For all iPhones and the iPod Touch

When it's time to clear your mind at the end of a day, music and meditation can do wonders. The Ambiscience Zen Master Bundle is actually two apps in one (Pure Meditation and Pure Yoga) and comes with 24 ambient music loops you can play through your headphones or iPhone speaker. The 20 entertainment effects (tones and beats) focus your mind so you can block out background noise to meditate like a master.

ZONE OUT: Even Zen Master's tracks have soothing names. If the sound of falling water relaxes you, try the loops called Evening Rain, A Gentle Thunderstorm, or Buddhist Rain, which layer the sound of showers over a synthesizer or chimes. The app lets you save your own volume presets so you don't have to fuss with levels every time you want to get Zen.

TRANCE TIMER: You don't have to stress yourself out watching the clock while you meditate. The app includes a built-in alarm clock that fades in with music, as well as a countdown timer to play the music for a specified number of minutes or hours before it gently fades out. You can also set a time on the clock to have the music automatically shut off.

Best App for Future Astronauts

NASA

Free
Version 1.24 | NASA Ames Research Center
For all iPhones and the iPod Touch

Space is still the final frontier, and this free, official app from the National Aeronautics and Space Administration keeps you informed of what's Out There—and how much of it NASA is involved with. The app details the agency's ventures, offering mission information, countdown clocks, launch schedules, and orbit trackers. It also offers NASA's gorgeous astronomy photos and videos, along with the administration's Twitter feeds.

MISSION POSSIBLE: NASA's app is as beautiful as the skies themselves. It's fun to flick through the administration's list of current missions and projects. Tap a mission name to get more information, as well as in-depth technical details about the spacecraft and subsystems involved. Tap the Images button to see NASA's Image of the Day.

ON THE LAUNCH PAD: Several NASA missions have yet to deploy, but the app provides plenty of backstory for what's going into space, where it's going, and what it's expected to do once it gets there. The buttons at the bottom of the screen let you see the NASA Twitter feeds directly related to that mission, as well as accompanying photos and videos.

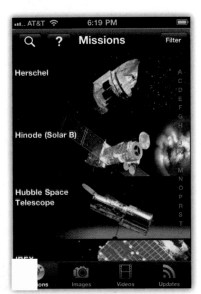

Best App for Busting Your Brain

The Moron Test
$0.99
Version 4.0 | Distinctive Dev Inc.
For all iPhones and the iPod Touch

It looks deceptively easy and innocent with its simple instructions inscribed on ancient-looking index cards, but wait until you get into The Moron Test. The game is an addictive series of challenges that fool you with home-grown graphics and then smacks you upside the head with trick questions and snarky comments about your lack of mental agility. The game has four sections, each with more than 100 steps to sharpen your reflexes.

PAY ATTENTION: The Moron Test starts out with a few extremely easy tasks, asking you to tap specific icons or put things in order, but then it starts throwing you curveballs, just hoping to trip you up in your own habits. The game forces you to read carefully and act accordingly.

LEFT BACK: When the game gets the better of you—and it usually does a few times before you start to anticipate its methods—you have to start over. Depending on how far you've gotten, this could be back at the beginning of the game, or at the start of the last level.

106

Best App for the Power of the Pen

The Elements of Style
$0.99
Version 5.2 | FrogLeap
For all iPhones and the iPod Touch

The classic little book of good grammar and English usage gets even smaller in this app—but still offers valuable advice for clear, focused writing. Known casually as "Strunk & White" (after creators William Strunk, Jr., and E.B. White), you can easily peruse the book's chapters or jump straight to any bookmarks you set. You can even boost the contrast by selecting white-on-black text.

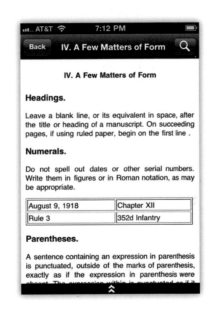

MODERN "STYLE": The Elements of Style app lays the groundwork for people who want to improve their writing skills. Get a better view of the app's text by tapping the arrows at the bottom of the screen to change the font style and size, along with the color of both the text and the background.

⊕ HONORABLE MENTION

Persuasive Writing Tips
$1.99
Version 1.0 | Nitin Gohel
For all iPhones and the iPod Touch

It doesn't have the iconic status that *The Elements of Style* has held for decades, but this app offers some good general advice for people who aren't used to communicating formally with the written word. The tips, which include short essays like "Do Not Inject Opinion" and "Write with Nouns and Verbs" are too basic for English majors, but may be helpful to others who suddenly find they have to write reports.

Best App for Thinking Outside the Box

Creative Whack Pack

$1.99
Version 4.1 | Creative Think
For all iPhones and the iPod Touch

Originally a deck of physical cards and now an offering in the App Store, Creative Whack Pack still serves its first purpose: to knock you out of the deep ruts of stodgy linear thinking patterns and encourage you to consider a problem from a new angle. Divided into four suits, just like playing cards or a Tarot deck, the Whack Pack has 64 strategies for finding creative new solutions to problems and keeps you entertained as you go.

PACK MENTALITY: When it feels like your brain has ground to a halt over a problem you've been mulling, take a whack at it with the Creative Whack Pack. The app's opening screen offers help from an electronic oracle or gives you a random idea to chew on. Some cards include sound effects to punctuate the illustrations and perhaps give you a little jolt.

SAGE ADVICE: If you choose to ask the Oracle, the app takes you to a screen that displays a menu of common issues. If you see your issue, tap it. If you don't, tap the I Have An Issue button and describe the problem. Like a gypsy fortune teller, the Oracle offers four cryptic mantras, like "See the Obvious" or "Combine Ideas," designed to goose your brain.

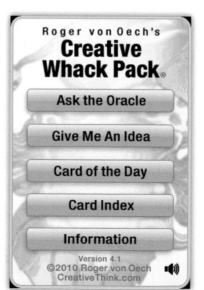

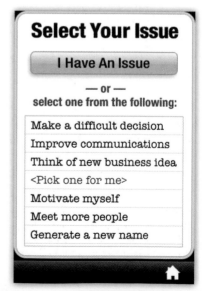

For Leisure

Ask "Why?"

2 Ask "Why?"

Stir your creative juices by asking why things are the way they are.

A good example is **Leonardo da Vinci** who said:

"I roamed the countryside searching for answers to things I did not understand.

"Why shells exist on the tops of mountains along with imprints of plants usually found in the sea.

"Why thunder lasts longer

19 Challenge the Rules

Improve communications

◀   NEXT   🏠

Q W E R T Y U I O P
A S D F G H J K L
⇧ Z X C V B N M ⌫
.?123   space   return

WELL-SUITED: The front of each Whack Pack card shows a simple drawing under a headline that's the same color as the card's border. The colors correspond to the Whack Pack's suits of Explorer, Artist, Judge, and Warrior. The suits represent the four types of thinking that go into the creative process and help you discover, transform, evaluate, and implement ideas.

SEND A CARD: Tap the icon in the middle of the toolbar to spin the card around so you can read the back. Here, you get a deeper explanation of the headline on the front, often supplemented by historic examples. If you find the card inspiring, tap the Share Card button at the top to email a copy to a friend or to post it on Facebook or Twitter.

HIDDEN NOTES: If the Whack Pack busts up your mental block and ideas come bursting out during an Oracle session, you don't have to scramble around for a notepad. The Oracle's cards each have a little turned-up bottom corner that reveals a hint of yellow notebook paper. Tap the corner and the keyboard pops up so you can jot down your ideas.

Best Apps For Play

Games are everywhere—on computers, on consoles, maybe even on your iPhone or iPod Touch. If you've ever spent more than five minutes in the App Store, you know it's bursting at the seams with thousands of pixelated pastimes. With so many games available, it can be hard to figure out what to play. That's where this chapter comes in.

Entertaining diversions come in all shapes and sizes, from **arcade games** that became legend as they gobbled your quarters at the mall to home console games that doubled your electric bill. This chapter introduces you to a few old friends, like Space Invaders, and to a lot of new ones, too.

For many people, e-pastimes are quieter affairs, like crossword or Sudoku **puzzles** that bend your brain and entertain at the same time. You'll find suggestions for those here, too. If table games come to mind, there are a couple of **gambling** apps, too.

The App Store has many more titles to offer, including **strategy games** for those who want to save the world or topple a king. Like football, basketball, or soccer? **Sports** games are just the ticket. And if your gaming tastes run to military adventures, this chapter suggests **combat games** and even a couple of **flights of fantasy**. Whether you're looking to kill time or aliens, this chapter has you covered. Turn the page to level up.

For Play

Best games for iPhone

download 'em all

Best App for a Space Invaders Remix

Space Invaders Infinity Gene
Free | $4.99 for full version
Version 3.0.0 | Taito Corp.
For all iPhones and the iPod Touch

One of the very first shoot-'em-up arcade games in the late 1970s, Space Invaders has landed in the App Store—with a surprising twist. You start out with the familiar cannon, blasting away at the advancing horde of aliens. But as you level up, the game evolves with stunning new visuals and challenging new aliens (even in the limited-level free version). You get a cool new movable cannon, too.

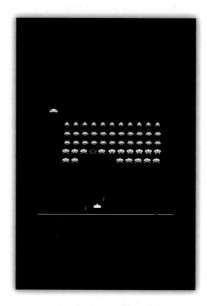

GOLDEN OLDIE: Space Invaders' first level will look familiar if you hung out at an arcade in the late 1970s. The objective is simple: use your finger to guide the gun back and forth and blast row after row of descending aliens. You can only move side-to-side, firing madly and dodging bombs until you blow them all away.

NEW SONG: Once you get past the first level, the game takes on a new look, with larger, more intense 3D aliens whipping by you. The game continues to evolve into something new with each level, but you always have the same objective: kill as many aliens as you can. You can play your own music in the background, too.

Best Pizza Parlor Classic Game

Wild West Pinball

$0.99
Version 2.6 | Gameprom Company
For all iPhones and the iPod Touch

Pizza parlors, bowling alleys, and video arcades just aren't as much fun unless there's a pinball machine around. If there's not, whip out your iPhone or iPod Touch loaded up with Wild West Pinball. Its nicely rendered 3D graphics and sound effects mimic the play on a full-size machine. To keep the ball ricochetting around the table, tilt your gadget just as you would a table in real life. Watch your play with the app's "live" or fixed camera.

YIPPIE-KI-YAY: With its Old West visuals and background music, Wild West Pinball has a quirky personality all its own and plays like a miniature version of its big glass-and-chrome inspiration. Tap the on-screen flippers to propel the ball back up the length of the table. You can use the classic multitouch pinch-and-spread moves to zoom in and out of the field of play.

⊕ HONORABLE MENTION

Glow Hockey 2

Free | $1.99 for full version
Version 2.2.0 | Natenai Ariyatrakool
For all iPhones and the iPod Touch

Air hockey tables were standard in pizza joints and arcades back in the '70s, and Glow Hockey 2 gives the classic two-player game a neon shimmer. The free version lets you knock the puck around against a computerized opponent, but the full version allows two players to compete head-to-head on the same iPhone or iPod Touch. Players in the paid version can also compete wirelessly on separate devices over Bluetooth or Wi-Fi.

Best Death Star Attack Game

Star Wars: Trench Run
$4.99
Version 2.0 | THQ Inc.
For all iPhones and the iPod Touch

Based on the exhilarating final battle scene in the classic 1977 movie, Star Wars: Trench Run puts you in the cockpit of a fighter ship, dodging Imperial TIE fighters while you navigate the Death Star's narrow trenches, avoiding cannon fire and random space junk. When playing in Dogfight mode, you can do battle using any one of five iconic ships, including a Y-wing and Darth Vader's own TIE fighter.

THAT'S NO MOON: One of the choices in your ship inventory is the Millennium Falcon, where you man the lower gun turret of the classic aircraft as you protect rebel fighters from incoming Imperial ships.

IN THE TRENCHES: Zoom along the surface of the Death Star or dogfight with the enemy. With a bit of Wi-Fi configuration, you can use your gadget as the controller for the web-based version of the game, too.

For Play

Best Retro 3D Game

Wolfenstein 3D
Classic Platinum

Free | $1.99 for full version
Version 1.3 | id Software
For all iPhones and the iPod Touch

The original Wolfenstein 3D game dates back to the days when MS-DOS roamed the desktop. Happily, the App Store's version revives all of Wolfenstein's chunky graphics and cold stone mazes. You play the part of OSA agent B.J. Blazkowicz, popping Nazis left and right as you roam the castle looking for hidden secrets—and a way out. The free version lets you play the first three levels of the full game.

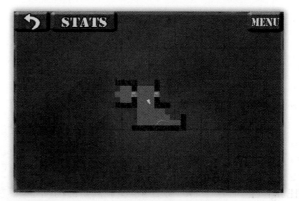

OLD AND NEW: The iPhone version of Wolfenstein includes the six original game episodes and 60 levels that grow increasingly more perilous as you proceed. The game takes advantage of the iPhone's tilt controls, letting you dive and dodge attackers.

ABOVE IT ALL: You'll spend a lot of the game navigating its maze of corridors, trying to find your way from room to room. To give you some perspective, tap the Maps button on the main screen to switch to an overhead view of your current location.

Best Vengeful Avian Game

Angry Birds

Free | $0.99 for full version
Version 1.4.0 | Rovio
For all iPhones and the iPod Touch

These aren't sweet songbirds squabbling over a turn at the feeder here—these birds are angry with a group of green pigs who invaded their nest, and they're going all-out for revenge. The highly addictive Angry Birds teaches a few lessons about trajectory and engineering as you catapult the birds toward the pigs, which are hiding in various structures. The free Lite version of the game lets you play 12 levels of hog-smashing fun.

SLING SHOT: After each bird hops into the catapult, pull back the band with your finger to take aim at the pigs residing on the other side of the screen. The dotted line shows the trajectory of the previous bird so you can adjust your aim.

HAM SANDWICH: By smashing into the weak part of a building, the birds methodically destroy the pigs' protective structures, exposing them. Once you squash or hit all the pigs, you move on to the next of the game's 165 levels.

Best Mythical Creature Action Game

Robot Unicorn Attack
$2.99
Version 1.0.3 | Cartoon Network
For all iPhones and the iPod Touch

Brought to you by the sardonic folks at Adult Swim (part of the Cartoon Network), Robot Unicorn Attack is highly silly—and very hard to put down at times. You, as the robot unicorn, gallop along the ground, leaping from floating cliff to floating cliff in the soft pastel sky. Rainbows, shimmering sparkles, and dolphins provide power-ups from time to time, and glass stars try to block your way.

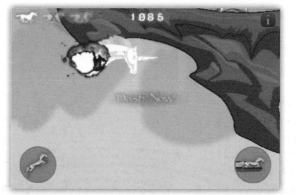

JUMP FOR JOY: Robot Unicorn's gameplay is simple. You gallop forward from cliff to cliff. Tap the left button to jump. Tap the right button to turbo-jump when you encounter a longer span (or an obstacle).

MOVING A HEAD: One mistimed jump or unavoided obstacle or glass star, and your unicorn meets a violent demise. As it plummets back to earth, its poor head flies across the screen like an unfortunate meteor.

Best Facebook Crossover Game

FarmVille

Free
Version 1.02 | Zynga
For all iPhones and the iPod Touch

Can't get enough of FarmVille on Facebook? This mobile app lets you play wherever you have a network connection, and it automatically updates your Facebook farm. If you don't already play on Facebook, you can start a fresh farm on your phone, but you have to have a Facebook account to do so. Like the original, the more you help your farming neighbors, the more quickly you advance in the game.

THE PLOT: Like all farms, you start out by planting seeds on a little patch of land and continue to grow virtual crops and raise cyber-livestock. You can invite friends to be your neighbors and earn "money" by helping out on other farms.

TO MARKET: As in real-life farming, you need to buy and sell crops and animals to advance. You earn the in-game currency, "farm coins," by selling you virtual crops. Use it to buy more seeds and livestock to expand your farming empire.

Best Undead Attack Game

Plants vs. Zombies

$2.99
Version 1.1 | PopCap Games
For all iPhones and the iPod Touch

PopCap Games, creators of Peggle, Bejeweled, and several other popular pastimes, scores again with this whimsical adventure. As zombies gather in the street to invade your house, you quickly plant layers of protective flora that attack the zombies as they advance. As more zombies lurch forward, you have to step up your game by catching turbo-growth sunbeams and planting seeds to fortify the ranks of your killer garden.

ZOMBIE JAMBOREE: The undead invaders start out on your street and begin to trudge toward your front door. Your goal is to keep them out of the house by planting up to 49 protective plants in your front yard, which grows increasingly lush over time.

GREEN ARMY: Tap the tiny suns as they float down to build up energy so you can feed more plants. In the early levels of the game, you plant pea-shooter seeds that grow up to blast advancing zombies with full-bore vegetable cannonballs.

Best Digital Dirigible Game

Blimp: The Flying Adventures

Free | $2.99 for full version
Version 1.0 | Smid Design s.r.o.
For all iPhones and the iPod Touch

Forget about slick spaceships—in Blimp, you pilot a woozy craft powered by hot air. You take it on a series of missions (pick up clients, bomb enemies) in an ethereally designed world that looks hand-painted. The app's full version offers more action than the sampler, which still gives you a feel for the game. Be sure to plug in your headphones to hear the clanking, banging audio effects and soundtrack.

For Play

FLYING COACH: As you might expect, learning to fly—and land—takes practice. Every pilot needs to hit the landing pad and pick up a passenger. It may take a few passes to land on the pad and not on your client (which tends to be bad for business).

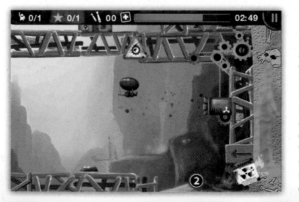

BLOWN AWAY: It's not all pie in the sky when you fly your digital blimp. Obstacles like blasting air vents can pelt you with particles and knock you off-course. Avoid the nasty fire jets as well or you'll see your little blimp go up in a smoking ball of flame.

Best Mindless Time-Killer

Paper Toss: World Tour

$0.99
Version 1.2 | Backflip Studios
For all iPhones and the iPod Touch

Tossing crumpled balls of paper into a wastepaper basket is a casual game that predates even that classic computerized time-waster, Solitaire. With no actual trees harmed in the making of its wadded balls, Paper Toss: World Tour offers a much more environmentally friendly way to practice your shot. It's a scenic travelogue as well, as your target appears in exotic locales around the world.

BASKET CASE: The app's rules don't vary much from the real-life office paper toss: flick your finger to lob a wad into the wastepaper basket. The on-screen arrow and number note the direction and strength of the wind. Hit three consecutive shots and you move on to the next level.

SANDS OF TIME: Wind isn't the only factor you have to cope with to get your ball into the can. As shown here in the Egyptian level, sandstorms can thwart your aim, too. The game brings you to eight locations (levels) worldwide. After that, a bonus location on a snowy ice floe awaits.

Best Ax-Wielding Puzzle Game

Alio the Woodcutter
$2.99
Version 1.1.3 | Lyxite
For all iPhones and the iPod Touch

The game Alio the Woodcutter looks deceptively simple: direct Alio's ax to chop down all the trees so he can return to his lumber truck. The game's rules add complications to this basic task, however. For example, Alio can't pass any fallen trees (unless they happen to be serving as bridges) and he can't cross over water. The game has more than 50 levels that require careful decisions about when and where to wield the ax.

CHOP SHOP: As these ghostly images show, trees only fall in the direction Alio faces, and they take up more or less space depending on their height. And because Alio can't pass over fallen trees, you need to plan your chopping carefully to avoid getting boxed in.

TREE TIPS: As you chop through the woods, the game flashes helpful hints on the lower part of the screen. The scoreboard at the top tells you how many more trees you need to cut down before you can advance to the next level. The Undo button reverses the effects of the ax.

For Play

Best Word Game

Words with Friends
Free | $2.99 for full version
Version 3.09 | Newtoy Inc.
For all iPhones and the iPod Touch

Online games where players compete to spell out words on a board with little letter tiles are all the rage on social networks (even if they aren't officially called "Scrabble"). Words with Friends falls into the same group. You can play with friends you know or friends you haven't met yet over the Internet and even do battle with a friend in the same room on the same device. Words with Friends' free version displays ads.

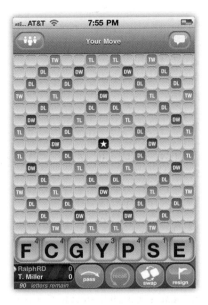

GAME TIME: Since the name of the game is Words with Friends, the first thing you need to do is find somebody to play against. You have four options: choose a player from your iPhone or iPod contacts list; pick somebody by user name who is also registered on the game's server; select a random online opponent; or choose Pass and Play for a local game.

TILE WORK: Once you pick your opponent, the game sets up the board. From there, the rules follow Scrabble: start in the center and drag the tiles in front of you to make a word or to add on to other words. The game is turn-based and not in real time, so you can have up to 20 matches going on at once; push notifications tell you when it's your turn.

Best Crossword Puzzle Game

2 Across
Free | $5.99 for full version
Version 2.0.3 | Eliza Block
For all iPhones and the iPod Touch

If you just can't get enough of those black-and-white word boxes, the full version of 2 Across is an excellent way to spend $6. Drawing from 26 sources around the world, the app puts thousands of crossword puzzles at your fingertips. And if you have a subscription to the *New York Times*, you can also download premium puzzles from its site. (The free Lite edition has a far smaller inventory, with just four puzzle sources to pick from.)

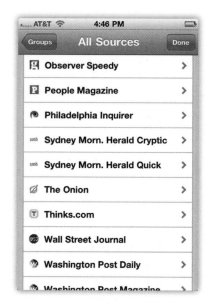

PUZZLE QUEST: Your first step is to pick a source for your puzzlement. The full version of 2 Across has crosswords from a range of publications, including *The Chronicle of Higher Education*, the *Toronto Globe and Mail*, England's *Manchester Evening News*, and even *People* magazine. Both the free and paid versions include puzzles from the humor rag *The Onion*.

DIGITAL INK: Some people brag about being so good at crosswords that they do them in ink. While typing doesn't really qualify as handwriting, you **can** choose the darker, more confident "pen" letters—or the lighter, more hesitant "pencil" text if you're cautiously working out the solutions. To choose, tap the relevant button at the top of the screen.

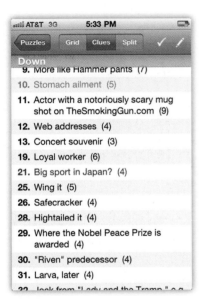

Crossword Puzzle Pro

Free | $5.99 for full version
Version 1.0.1 | Burda Social Brands GmBH
For all iPhones and the iPod Touch

Crossword Puzzle Pro doesn't quite have the inventory of 2 Across, but it gets points for a nice interface that conserves space by wedging the clues into the "black" boxes on the grid. When you start a puzzle, you choose from three skill levels (Normal, Difficult, or Genius), each with an increasingly more obscure vocabulary. The app's full version has 600 puzzles waiting to engage your brain, while the free edition has 9 to solve.

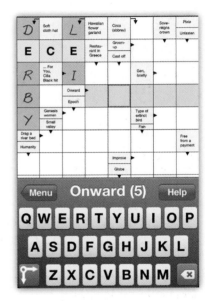

Best Sudoku Game

The New York Times Sudoku Daily

$2.99
Version 1.0.0 | Magmic Inc.
For all iPhones and the iPod Touch

Sudoku means "single number" in Japanese, and that's the goal of the game that's been mesmerizing international puzzle fans for the past few years. You have nine small 3 × 3 grids inside a larger grid, and you somehow have to get every number from 1 to 9 in each row and column, no repeats allowed. The app holds 5,000 *New York Times* Sudoku puzzles, and you can download a new one each day.

PUZZLE PALS: Sudoku Daily offers five difficulty levels. Rank newbies probably want to stick with the Easy level. From there, the levels ascend to Medium to Hard to Super, then reach their apex at Genius. Serious Sudoku players can compete against each other in online leaderboards or send messages comparing the time it took to crack a puzzle.

SCARLET NUMBER: If you need a little affirmation or just want to see how badly you're doing in a current grid, tap the checkmark button in the top-right corner. The app highlights Incorrect answers in a very noticeable red, giving you the chance to rethink your choices and make corrections. Be forewarned that the clock above the grid keeps ticking, however.

For Play

NEWS BITS: In an obtrusive bit of cross-branding in the Extras menu, the app displays a tiny image of the front page of the current day's *New York Times*. If any of the headlines catch your eye, tap the page, and then tap Yes to visit the paper's mobile website. (This book's author works on the *Times*' Book Review, but has nothing to do with the puzzle people.)

Enjoy Sudoku

Free | $2.99 for full version
Version 3.4.2 | Jason T. Linhart
For all iPhones and the iPod Touch

This aptly named app is for people who really love Sudoku and just can't get enough of those alluring 81 squares. With 16 difficulty levels and its own puzzle generator to keep 'em coming, you may never run out of fresh grids with the full version of Enjoy Sudoku. (Using the built-in camera, iPhone owners can even snap and scan puzzles from newspapers.) The free version has fewer puzzles and 14 difficulty levels, but that may be enough for you.

CLOUD NINE: Practiced Sudoku fans can joyfully whip out the grids in no time, but players new to the world of Sudoku may need more time—and a little bit of help. If you find yourself constantly hitting the Erase button, you can take a peek at the solution by tapping the Hint button. Tiny numbers appear in the squares to clue you in on the solution.

Best Maze Game

Dark Nebula

$0.99
Version 1.1 | 1337 Game Design
For all iPhones and the iPod Touch

Maze games have been around forever, but few look as sleek and polished as Dark Nebula. The first of several planned "episodes," this app has 10 levels where you guide a disk (which looks like a Roomba robotic vacuum cleaner) through a 3D labyrinth using all the moves in the iPhone accelerometer's arsenal. Unlike many games, you don't even have to touch the screen here—you do all your gameplay by tilting.

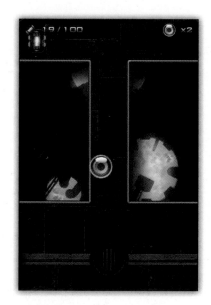

LONG WAY DOWN: In addition to twisting corridors, sliding obstacles, and glowing barriers, Dark Nebula has you navigate a little round robot across very narrow bridges. If you tilt your phone a little too far, you go hurtling off the edge of the structure and into the fiery pits below. If you have extra lives left, you pick up not far from where you took the plunge.

GAME OF LIFE: Dark Nebula smartly complements its graphics with stirring background music and realistic sound effects. Roll over enough glowing yellow cylinders and you get an extra life, which keeps you playing even if you do go headfirst off a bridge. When you finish all 10 levels of this episode, look for Episode Two in the App Store.

Best Third-Dimension Game

3D Puzzle

$1.99
Version 1.0 | Nanjing Imohoo IT Co. Ltd.
For all iPhones and the iPod Touch

This game challenges you to make sense out of a series of floating colored squares and figure out at which angle they need to be to create a mosaic picture. When the disembodied tiles appear, drag an area with your finger to shift the whole mass in that direction. As you drag, the squares move in relation to each other until you hit the magic angle and the picture appears. 3D Puzzle has four modes of difficulty and 500 pictures.

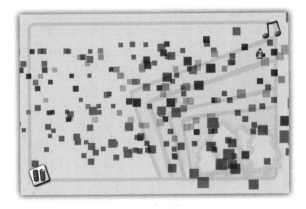

SQUARE ROOTS: Depending on the angle, 3D Puzzle's floating boxes may start to look like something—or bring to mind a cloud of digital confetti. A tiny image in the upper-right corner of the screen offers a clue to the picture you're trying to see.

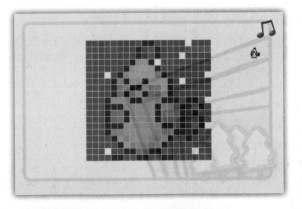

CUBISM: Once all the squares fall into alignment, the mosaic reveals itself. The game has several types of pictures, including images of animals, plants, and toys. Tap the music-note icon in the upper-right to pick your own tunes to play in the background.

Best Online Poker Game

World Series of Poker: Hold 'Em Legend
$0.99
Version 1.6.0 | Glu Mobile Inc.
For all iPhones and the iPod Touch

A table full of poker players can be hard to squeeze onto an iPhone, but the World Series of Poker's app brings a compact and well-designed look to the high-stakes game. Six or nine players—including you—are seated around a table playing Hold 'Em. You can play in real time against Internet opponents, or you can play against the app. Play well, and the game recognizes you with escalating awards.

For Play

TABLE TOUR: The World Series of Poker takes you around the world. When you start the game, you choose where you want to play, including a virtual 5th Street Pub or Harrah's New Orleans. Other casinos become available as you accumulate chips.

WHEEL OF FORTUNE: Eliminating players from the table requires some creative controls. When it's your turn to bet, tap your chip stack to call up the app's money dial. Choose the amount you want to put in and then tap the checkmark to place your bet.

CARD COACH: Novice Texas Hold 'Em players can get guidance from right within the app. The height of the rainbow-themed meter next to your cards indicates the strength of your hand—and it can help you decide what to do when it's your turn.

KNOW YOUR PLACE: In the Stats area, you can see how you're doing at the table. Tap the Player option on the game's main menu and flick through to Stats. In addition to seeing your current cash and ranking, the screen displays your best hand.

Live Poker 7K Free

Free
Version 3.7 | Zynga
For all iPhones and the iPod Touch

Zynga, the company that makes the FarmVille app described earlier in this chapter, also makes an online "live" poker game for the iPhone and iPod Touch. In fact, you can *only* play the game online and only against other people, but for many folks, that's the whole point. Live Poker 7K is popular on social-networking sites, and Facebook users can sign into their account through the app, and then invite and play with fellow Facebookers. With 6 million daily players, you should always be able to find a free seat.

Best Real-Time Strategy Game

Land Air Sea Warfare

$4.99
Version 1.1 | 244 Graphics LLC
For all iPhones and the iPod Touch

World-builders and armchair generals alike can spend hours inside real-time strategy games. In Land Air Sea Warfare, you pick your terrain, establish a base of operations (barracks, power plants, and so on), and eventually command a mighty army into battle against the enemy (Russia). Once you conquer your foe (or surrender), you can build up your war machine on a different landscape.

POWER UP: Although you can soon expand your base of operations with buildings and other structures, you need to harness some energy and build up power first. Tap the Engr button to place wind turbines or other power sources around your base.

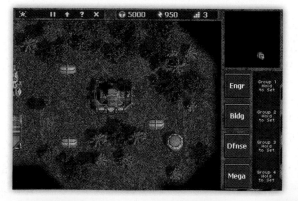

WAR MACHINE: As you pull in energy, you can begin building defenses—and offenses. Add munitions factories to crank out ships, planes, and transport units, and eventually attack your enemy in a hail of explosions and sound effects.

Best Sliding-Puzzle Strategy Game

Warship: Flight Deck Jam

$0.99
Version 1.0 | Demansol
For all iPhones and the iPod Touch

In Flight Deck Jam, you're in charge of an aircraft carrier's crowded flight deck, and it's your job to keep it operational so your fighter jets can take off. The game has two modes, Relax and Challenge. Relax gives you time to leisurely move your armored gear around while a chopper guards you, but you need to step it up in Challenge mode because the enemy fires missiles while you work.

JAMMED UP: Warship starts with the flight deck filled with planes, tanks, and trucks—and limited space. You need to figure out how to shift everything around so the orange plane can take off—but the trucks, tanks, and planes' movement is limited.

OPEN RUNWAY: Warship's weapons can only move in a straight line, and only in the direction they face, so you have to figure out how to move your hardware up and down and side to side to solve the puzzle. Eventually, you clear the way for the jet.

133

Best Tower Defense Game

Sentinel 2: Earth Defense
$1.99
Version 1.4.2 | Origin8 Technologies Ltd.
For all iPhones and the iPod Touch

A sequel to Sentinel: Mars Defense, Sentinel 2 brings the action back to earth as rampaging aliens try to make rubble of your turrets. Rich graphics and music pull you into the gameplay as you place towers around the landscape to defend your turf. Other weapons in your arsenal include an orbiting laser and mobile drones that attack the aliens (and keep you entertained).

GAME CONSOLE: The game's main screen has all the controls you need to customize your experience. Sentinel 2, like any other iPhone game, supports OpenFeint, an online gaming network that lets you play against friends, chat with fellow gamers, and track high scores.

WEAPONS GRADE: The invading aliens have to navigate the Earth's unfamiliar landscape, buying you some time to get your defenses in order. As you play, you can upgrade to more deadly towers and other weapons, but you have to manage your resources wisely.

PLAY ON: The game includes a soundtrack by Specimen A, but you can play along to your own music. Tap the Music button on the game's main screen (opposite page, top) to call up a variation of the On-the-Go playlist. Scroll through and tap the songs you want to put on your Sentinel playlist, and then tap Done to hear the tunes in the game.

GeoDefense Swarm
$1.99
Version 1.5 | Critical Thought Games LLC
For all iPhones and the iPod Touch

Because they don't require a lot of complex input, tower defense games work great on touch-screens—and there are a lot of great tower defense games *for* the touchscreen. GeoDefense Swarm has quite a different look to it than Sentinel 2, but it brings its own intense action to the genre. Specialty structures, like the shockwave-harnessing Thump Tower and the powerful Vortex Tower, add to your defenses.

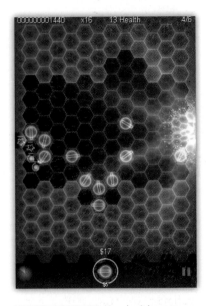

TOWER OF POWER: You don't have to build your towers along twisting paths or other rugged terrain in GeoDefense Swarm—you can create clusters of towers to blast invaders. The game has six types of towers and 30 levels of gameplay to keep you busy. For newbies to the world of tower defense, GeoDefense Swarm includes helpful tutorials.

135

Best Chess Game

Fritz Chess
$4.99
Version 1.4 | Gammick Entertainment
For all iPhones and the iPod Touch

Fritz, a German computer chess program first developed in the 1990s, has played against both Garry Kasparov and an early version of IBM's Deep Blue computer—and now you can have a version of the software in your pocket. Fritz Chess is challenging to play against, but it's also a wonderful resource to help you improve your game. It includes a database of 100,000 historic matches, a help system, and tools to analyze your moves.

CHECK, MATE: You can drag and drop your pieces around the chess board, or jump to squares by tapping them. You can also undo a move by shaking your iPhone or Touch. The game gives you your choice of chessboard and music, and there are various ways to play against other people, including a two-player mode. You can also email games in chess notation.

GRAND MASTER: Fritz is a great app for learning chess, and its in-game help provides hints and visual clues. For example, it can alert you to pieces threatened by your opponent by highlighting the board squares. Chess is an ancient game with plenty of history, and Fritz even tells you the name of your first move, like the Reti or Durkin's Opening.

Best Checkers Game

Checkers!

Free | $1.99 for full version
Version 1.2.4 | OutOfTheBit
For all iPhones and the iPod Touch

Checkers is one of the first board games many people learn to play, but the rules can vary depending on *where* you learned to play. Checkers lets you play by the English, Spanish, Italian, or French rules, with your choice of five checkerboard color schemes. You can interrupt your game with text messages or phone calls without losing your moves. The free version clutters the top of the board with ads.

SET 'EM UP: In Checkers, you play against the app or a live person. Tap the Settings icon to customize the game with each player's name. You can also choose the checker colors, turn the sound effects on or off, and pick the rules by which you wish to play (the variations tend to involve the movement allowed by kings).

BUST A MOVE: Once you choose your settings, the game begins and you can start jumping your way around the board. You can see your chosen set of rules and difficulty level at the top of the screen if you're playing against the program. If you want to change them, jump back into the settings area.

Best Soccer Game

FIFA 10
$6.99
Version 1.3 | Electronic Arts Inc.
For all iPhones and the iPod Touch

Whether you call it footie, fútbol, or soccer, the so-called "beautiful game" looks truly gorgeous in FIFA 10. FIFA, the Fédération Internationale de Football Association, is the governing body of global soccer, and the game it's produced with Electronic Arts uses real teams in real leagues to make the game more fun as you work toward your goal (which is, of course, the goal). As in the real-life game, you can even compete in tournaments.

HEAD-TO-HEAD: On-screen game controls get you in the game as you charge out of midfield and make your way toward your opponent's goalkeeper. You can view the match from six angles and play against a friend over a local Wi-Fi connection.

FOR KICKS: In a penalty shoot-out, you trade off kicking and defending the net, guiding the action with your finger. The stadium has a realistic feel, right down to the flashing banners along the sides and the roar of the rowdy crowd in the stands.

Best Basketball Game

Crazy Basketball

$0.99
Version 4.0 | Demis Mezirov
For all iPhones and the iPod Touch

Aim is one thing, but you definitely need the right touch to nail buckets in Crazy Basketball. Like a pocket version of Pop-a-Shot, the game gives you a set amount of time to make as many baskets as you can, but it's not as easy as it looks; flick the ball too abruptly and it slams off the backboard. The game has realistic sound effects, down to the clank of the rim and smack of the ball on the polished wood "court."

SLAM-DUNK: Crazy Basketball has three playing levels (Easy, Normal, and Hard) so it can help entertain younger fingers without frustrating them. A dotted line with a suggested trajectory helps you line up your shots as the clock ticks down.

TROPHY CASE: The game can connect to the OpenFeint network so you can share your high scores with other players, but you also have the chance to earn local awards for your shooting skills. Tap the Achievements button on the main screen to see the rewards.

Best Golf Game

Anytime Golf: Magic Touch

$0.99
Version 1.3 | Bork 3D LLC
For all iPhones and the iPod Touch

One thing about playing video golf: You don't have to worry about the weather. Anytime Golf: Magic Touch brings blue skies and a light breeze to your screen on several 3D courses. The game gives you plenty of control, from picking your clubs for each shot to switching between overhead views of the hole and the player's perspective. A virtual driving range lets you practice whacking balls.

SWING DANCE: You hit a ball by dragging your fingertip vertically down the screen for the backswing and then flicking it up in the direction you want the ball to go for the downswing. Good control makes for a more accurate shot, while fidgety fingers can land you in the rough—so take your time and aim carefully.

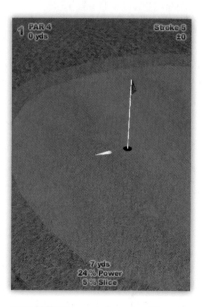

GO GREEN: The top-left corner of the screen shows the current hole number and par rating. The top-right corner shows the number of strokes it took to get to the digital green. Once you get close to the cup, pick up your virtual putter and gently flick your finger toward the flag to finish off this hole and move on to the next.

Best Football Game

Backbreaker Football

Free | $0.99 for full version
Version 1.5 | NaturalMotion Games Ltd.
For all iPhones and the iPod Touch

With all the bone-rattling action and none of the actual physical pain (unless you get sore fingers), Backbreaker Football is a great way to while away the time between real pigskin games—or their commercials. You get to design your own player down to his name, and then send him out to dodge the opposing team's defense in a mad run toward the end zone, a task that gets harder as you advance in the game.

IN-FLIGHT MOVIE: If you're not fast enough to dodge your opponent, your virtual player ends up much like the real guys do—flying headfirst through the air. When you do get tackled, the game replays it from several angles, just like on TV.

END ZONE: Use the game's controls to spin and sprint your way past the opposing team to score a virtual TD. Master the game's basics and move on to one of Backbreaker Football's Challenge modes. Complete a challenge, and you unlock new content.

Best Car-Racing Game

Real Racing
$4.99
Version 1.23 | Firemint
For all iPhones and the iPod Touch

In Real Racing, the iPhone and iPod Touch's built-in accelerometer turns your device into a racecar steering wheel. You're in the driver's seat and you can keep that perspective or switch to a less intense external view as you roar around the racetrack. If you have a Wi-Fi network and a bunch of iPhone-equipped friends who also own a copy of Real Racing, the game's multiplayer mode lets six of you race at once.

ON TRACK: To start racing, pick your car and track—your options increase the more you play. Keeping the car on the track can be a challenge for inexperienced players, but, fortunately, smacking into a wall or lurching off the track only slows you down.

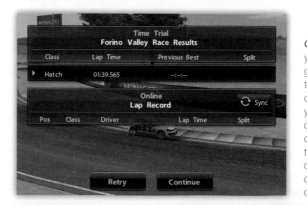

CLOCK SPEED: Once you finish a race, the game displays your time and the type of car you were driving so you can see how you did. If you're using the cockpit view during the race, the app also displays your lap time on the car's dashboard clock, shown above.

Best App for Fantasy Teams

Fantasy Monster

Free | $3.99 for full version
Version 1.3 | Bignoggins Productions LLC
For all iPhones and the iPod Touch

Fantasy sports (also known to some as *rotisserie*) involves creating an imaginary team out of real players. You use the real-life statistics of those players in a point system to compete against other fantasy team owners in a fantasy season. Yahoo runs one of the biggest fantasy sports websites, and Fantasy Monster lets you manage your Yahoo teams while you're on the go so you can keep tabs on the team's performance and standing.

SPORTING NEWS: Fantasy league play follows the real-life sports leagues closely. For those on a quest to build a championship team, Fantasy Monster compiles plenty of information so you can choose wisely when you draft and trade players.

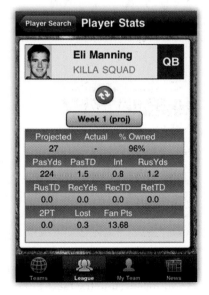

DREAM TEAM: The on-the-field performance of real-life players is key to having a successful sports fantasy team, so fantasy-league owners tend to have an even more obsessive love of statistics than more casual sports fans.

Best Fantasy Combat Game

Predators
$3.99
Version 1.3 | Fox Digital Entertainment
For all iPhones and the iPod Touch

Action-packed and not for the squeamish, Predators casts you as a hunted alien trying to survive against a pack of murderous humans. You're not a defenseless creature, though; a set of Wolverine-like razor claws can slice and dice your attackers. Due to Predators' gore and violence, the game is rated for those age 12 and up. After a long day in the office or out on sales calls, Predators can be an engaging bit of stress relief.

BUTTON DOWN: Similar to console controllers, Predators' touchscreen offers virtual buttons so you can direct your avatar and control his razor claws and plasma guns. In the early levels of the game, you do a lot of clawing.

BLOOD BANK: A companion to the 2010 *Predators* movie, the mobile game, like the movie, doesn't skimp on the graphic violence. If you find it getting to you, you can turn off the spurting blood in the game's Options settings.

Best Historical Combat Game

Great Tank War

$2.99
Version 1.0.0 | Jellyoasis Inc.
For all iPhones and the iPod Touch

Even back in the chocky-blocky days of the Atari 2600, a good tank program could entertain for hours. Great Tank War brings 3D graphics and easy-to-learn controls to the armored-vehicle genre and makes it all work on your iPhone or iPod Touch screen. You command historically accurate World War II-era tanks against the German army's Tiger tanks (and other war machines) in a fierce battle to beat the Nazis in occupied Europe.

THINK TANK: The game uses the classic "two-stick shooter" method of play, where you have one control for movement and one for firing your weapons as you figure out how to beat the enemy. As you play, you can upgrade your tank's armor and weapons to mow down Nazis.

⊕ HONORABLE MENTION

Battle of WWII

Free | $6.99 for full version
Version 1.6.0 | Simubiotic GmbH
For the iPhone 3G, 3GS, and 4
and the iPod Touch 2G and 3G

The Battle of Normandy was a turning point in World War II, and this game puts you right in the 9th Division to battle your way across northern France. It's a real-time strategy game, so you need to keep an eye on resources as you battle across the realistic landscapes. You set up attacks with your infantrymen, tanks, and artillery for 12 different missions and 14 maps in the paid version; the free edition offers two missions and one map to give you a feel for the game.

Best Flight Simulator

X-Plane Extreme
$9.99
Version 9.551 | Laminar Research
For all iPhones and the iPod Touch

A sequel to the popular X-Plane 9 flight simulator, X-Plane Extreme continues its predecessor's sophisticated look and feel. The app gives you the chance to virtually pilot realistic recreations of the F-22 Raptor, the SR-71 Blackbird, the B-2 bomber and other modern jets. In addition to enjoying the scenic views as you soar through the sky, you can race other planes across the terrain, which includes plenty of mountains and canyons.

TOP GUN: During takeoff, you increase the plane's speed with the throttle slider on the left and slow things down with the flap control on the right. Tilt your gadget to steer the aircraft, just like you do in a racing game.

SIM CITY: X-Plane Extreme offers a full menu of options for simulated flight. In addition to picking the type of plane you want to fly, you can choose other options to suit your gameplay, like the time of day or region you fly over.

Best Space Combat Simulator

Space Wars 3D Star Combat Simulator

$1.99
Version 1.0 | Robert Bennett
For all iPhones and the iPod Touch

If you prefer your simulated flight in a more fanciful realm, Space Wars 3D combines a shooting game with a galactic flight simulator. The game lets you jump into the cockpit of a star fighter in the Human Space Navy and take out a few enemy aliens—if they don't blast you to bits first. You can pick your own ship before you begin your mission and you even earn "money" for fighting.

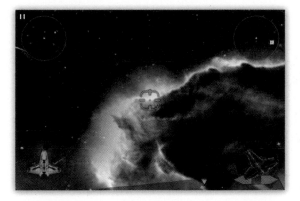

GALAXY QUEST: Space Wars has beautiful graphics, from the rugged star fighters to the lovely views as you fly into battle. The controls are simple: steer with your left thumb on the glass, and shoot with your right thumb when you see an enemy ship.

UNDER FIRE: The enemy ships get to shoot, too, and flashing red means you're getting fragged. You can take a few hits before your shields give out, but you need to maneuver around and take out your attacker before you end up floating home.

Best Apps At Home

Business tool, entertainment machine, eReader, social secretary—you might think that your iPhone serves best outside the home, but that's not the case. As this chapter reveals, with the right apps, your iPhone or iPod Touch edges you toward domestic bliss, too.

In many households, the kitchen is a focal point, from the start of the day through dinner, when the family gathers around the communal table. Read on for apps that get you **cooking** in style and that help you make healthy choices when you do. If you're attending to **shopping and errands**, apps can help make finding the product you're looking for easier and more efficient.

Recent economic conditions may have you concerned about finances, and apps that help you **manage your money** can show you where every penny goes.

Although it can't save you some dough by serving as a full-fledged babysitter, the iPhone has apps that work well to **distract the kids**, whether you're trapped in line at a store or at home whipping up a 20-minute meal.

And if you're the type who spends a lot of time in your personal castle and want to make it even nicer, apps that focus on **home work**—assignments to improve your domicile—can help get you there.

Best App for Healthy Recipes

Healthy Recipes
Free
Version 1.0.1 | SparkPeople Inc.
For all iPhones and the iPod Touch

If you're looking for recipes that offer light, tasty fare, Healthy Recipes lives up to its name. With more than 190,000 dishes to search or browse through, odds are you'll find *something* for dinner that won't load you down with nitrates and trans fats. And if one of your goals for healthy eating is to lose some lard, Healthy Recipes lists each dish's calories and carbs, percentage of fat, and other nutritional data.

SLICE AND DICE: If you yearn for a certain food, say couscous, you can search Healthy Recipes for dishes that use that ingredient. You can also filter the collection by total calories, prep time, type of ethnic cuisine (you'll see that German food doesn't *need* to be heavy), and more. You can browse by dietary needs, too, like vegetarian, gluten-free, and lactose-free dishes.

SHARE YOUR FOOD: When you find a dish you just have to share with foodie friends, email a link to the recipe with a tap of the Share button; the auto-generated message includes a plug for *SparkRecipes.com*, the parent site of this free app. Tap the View Online button to load Safari and see a recipe online, along with comments from other cooks.

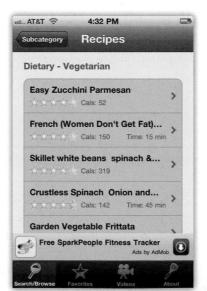

TV DINNER: Tap Healthy Recipe's Videos button to find recipes that include a multimedia cooking lesson. In these brief 5- or 10-minute clips, Chef Meg guides you through dish preparation, offering helpful kitchen tips as she goes along. Healthy Recipes stores the video lessons on YouTube's website, so you'll need a network connection to see them.

The Betty Crocker Mobile Cookbook
Free
Version 2.0.1 | General Mills Inc.
For all iPhones and the iPod Touch

This fictional household legend first appeared in the early 1920s, and Betty Crocker is still making her mark as a kitchen whiz 90 years later. The portable edition of the famous Betty Crocker Cookbook lets you search 9,000 recipes so you can keep your meals varied. If you have a taste for a certain food, say eggplant, browse the app by main ingredient. Haven't had time to grocery shop this week? Type in the contents of your cupboard and Betty displays recipes that use those ingredients.

MODERN MODIFICATIONS: The Betty Crocker Cookbook has been around for decades, so not every recipe is for the health-conscious. The app includes a recipe for "Awesome Banana Split Pancakes," for example, which probably isn't on the Weight Watchers list of approved foods. Still, you can find plenty of dishes that have been "healthified" for lower fat and calories.

Best App for Pocket Cooking Lessons

20 Minute Meals
$7.99
Version 1.2 | Zolmo Ltd.
For all iPhones and the iPod Touch

Affable British chef Jamie Oliver brings 60 of his inventive recipes to this beautifully designed app. Mixing video, full-screen photographs, and voice-overs with a bright, easy-to-use interface, the app teaches you how to make pasta, stir-fry, risotto, curry, and other worldly dishes. You also get videos that demonstrate essential kitchen skills, and you can add the ingredients for a recipe you like to a built-in shopping list with the tap of a button.

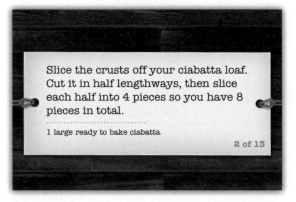

Slice the crusts off your ciabatta loaf. Cut it in half lengthways, then slice each half into 4 pieces so you have 8 pieces in total.

1 large ready to bake ciabatta

2 of 13

BITE SIZE: Oliver breaks down each recipe into short, numbered steps, displayed in big type. Once you complete a step, swipe the screen to move on to the next one. In portrait mode, you can scroll through the steps.

Sweet French toast with marmalade sauce

SEE AND DO: If you follow a recipe in landscape view, double-tap the screen to flip over the recipe "card" for a photo of what you should be doing at this point. As you swipe along, you may get some surprise audio advice from Oliver.

Best App for Nutritional Information

Nutrition Menu

$0.99
Version 1.25.1 | Shroomies LLC
For all iPhones and the iPod Touch

You can keep a close eye on what you ingest when you have nutritional information on more than 41,000 restaurant meals and 51,000 grocery staples at your fingertips. Nutrition Menu records and totals your daily nutritional intake (calories, carbs, fats, and so on) and lists your food score (a customizable tally for diets that track a single number). On the rare chance you don't find a food listed, you can add the information yourself.

BY THE NUMBERS: Along with menu items from 356 restaurant chains in the US and Canada, Nutrition Menu lists the nutrients in thousands of popular brand-name foods. Add a food item to your daily intake log with a tap of the Add to Journal button, and bookmark frequently gobbled foods with the Add to Favorite button so you can easily access them.

BURN NOTICE: Watching what you eat isn't just about intake—Nutrition Menu counts outgoing calories as well. Tap the Exercises button to see activities you engage in (from aerobics to yoga) and their calorie burn. The app factors in these negative calories along with the calories you consume, and displays a daily report of your caloric and nutritional intake.

Best App for Mall Shopping

ShopStyle Mobile
Free
Version 2.3 | Sugar Publishing Inc.
For all iPhones and the iPod Touch

If you can't get to the mall right now, bring the mall to you with ShopStyle Mobile, a mega-catalog for most department stores and designers. You can search for clothing (both adults' and kids'), accessories, household items, and more by store, brand, or category (like baby gear or men's jeans). If you need a second opinion, tap the envelope icon to email a picture and description to a friend—or post them to Facebook and Twitter.

SHOPPORTUNITY: ShopStyle Mobile is perfect for window-shopping—even if that window is your 3.5-inch touchscreen. When you see a picture of an item you like, tap it to get more information. If you're feeling impulsive and don't want to see the item live in the store (or try it on), tap the Buy button to go to the seller's website and complete your purchase.

At Home

HONORABLE MENTION

Mall Maps Mobile
Free
Version 1.01 | V.B. & Smith LLC
For all iPhones and the iPod Touch

When it comes time to hit the mall in person, this app guides the way—not only to the mall itself, but, once you get there, to all the stores in the mall. Mall Maps Mobile diagrams store locations and lists store directories for malls around the country. You can use location services to find the mall closest to you right now, or browse a list of malls in towns you plan to visit. Tap the name of a store to call ahead and see if they have what you want.

Best App for Rocking Craigslist

CraigsPro
Free | $0.99 for full version
Version 3.004 | IOCo
For all iPhones and the iPod Touch

Craigslist, which began life in 1995 as a local-events email list, quickly expanded from its humble beginnings to become the classified advertising hub of the Earth. The CraigsPro app (free with ads sprinkled throughout) pares down Craigslist listings so you can see a screenfull of classifieds on your mobile device. You can look for jobs, apartments, and goods in multiple cities, post your own listings, and save your frequent searches.

MASSIVE MARKETPLACE: No matter what you're looking for, someone, somewhere is selling it on Craigslist (or will be soon). When you start the app, pick the city or cities you want to search and then pick the category you're interested in, like Auto Parts. CraigsPro displays the classified listings in a scrolling list, with the asking price highlighted in red on the right side of the listing.

CLASSIFIED INFORMATION: Just like the old tiny-text newspaper ads, each CraigsPro listing provides contact info for the seller and a description of what they're selling, renting, or providing as a service. Tap the Details button to see the original Web posting or to plot the listed location on a map. You can add the listing to a Favorites list, share it with your Twitter followers, or email it.

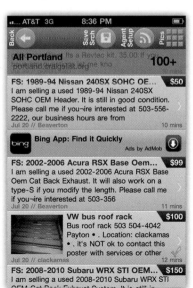

155

Best App for Online Deals

PriceGrabber

Free
Version 1.3.1 | PriceGrabber
For all iPhones and the iPod Touch

Thanks to the Web, comparison shopping has never been easier, and this app brings the power of *PriceGrabber.com*, the Web's popular price-comparison site, to the small screen. Type in the name of a product you're looking for and the app displays the best prices—including tax and shipping—from online stores. You can browse customer reviews of the product and check out merchant ratings before you buy, too.

BAR-GAINS: Standing in a store wondering if you can find the same thing for less on the Web? Scan the item's barcode with your iPhone's camera (or tap in the numbers by hand), and PriceGrabber translates the code to a product name and displays price comparisons from competing merchants. If you find a better deal online, tap the Shop button to buy it.

⊕ **HONORABLE MENTION**

WootWatch

Free
Version 1.5.1 | David Rahardja
For all iPhones and the iPod Touch

"Woot" is an old text-chat expression that conveys enthusiastic joy. *Woot.com* is an e-commerce site with the slogan "One Day, One Deal." Its daily bargain could be anything from a PC to a funky lawn sprinkler. Whatever it is, WootWatch profiles it with a delightfully snarky description (scroll down) in a clean, colorful interface. The app has running daily deals for wine, t-shirts, and toys, too. Tap the "I Want One!" button to pay up at the Woot site.

At Home

Shopping

156

Best App for Car Maintenance

Car Minder Plus
$2.99
Version 3.1.2 | Joshua Monroe
For all iPhones and the iPod Touch

Forget those paper logbooks crammed into your glove compartment. Car Minder Plus records your car's day-to-day needs and its long-term service history. You can set maintenance reminders by date or mileage, and the app includes a gas log so you can figure your miles-per-gallon rating and graph it over time. If you're managing the household motor pool, the app keeps records for all your cars.

AUTO REMINDER: Preventive care can keep your ride out of the repair shop. When you set up Car Minder Plus, add maintenance routines that you regularly perform, like oil changes and tire rotations, to the list. When your car needs service, relevant items in Car Minder's Service List go red.

FIX LIST: Car Minder lets you record unplanned trips to the shop, too. When you take your car in, log the date, odometer reading, and type of repair. When the list gets too long or the repairs come too frequently, it may be time to consider a sale, trade-in, or sad trip to rust-bucket Valhalla.

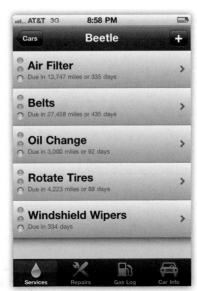

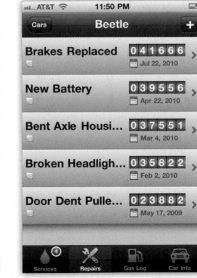

Best App for Tracking Your Finances

Pageonce Personal Finance

Free | $6.99 for full version
Version 3.83 | Pageonce Inc.
For all iPhones and the iPod Touch

Need a dashboard for money-related activities? Pageonce Personal Finance lets you keep tabs on all your financial accounts in one place. Manage bills, bank accounts, credit cards, stock portfolios, and more on the go. The Premium app updates all your accounts with a single tap. Paid version or ad-supported freebie, Pageonce uses tough encryption technology to protect your sensitive information.

ACCOUNTING 101: When you launch Pageonce, its Let's Get Started screen invites you to add accounts, prompting you with common brand names like AmEx, AT&T, Wells Fargo, and Gmail. Tap the More button to get forms for companies not listed. To add an account, enter your user name and password for financial institutions, frequent flier clubs, and other accounts.

DIVERSIFIED PORTFOLIO: Along with accounts for banks, credit cards, brokerage firms, utilities, airlines, hotel rewards clubs, and popular e-commerce sites like Amazon and eBay, you can add email and social accounts to Pageonce's roster. Once you log in, the app tracks status updates, feeds, new email messages, and Skype credit (for calls and services that Skype charges for).

158

⊕ HONORABLE MENTION

Mint.com

Free
Version 1.4 | Mint.com
For all iPhones and the iPod Touch

If you want to focus purely on finances, *Mint.com*'s mobile app is all about money management. You need to set up an account on the website (now owned by Intuit, makers of Quicken personal finance software). Once you provide your banking and investment info, the app syncs up with your financial institutions each day and displays all your info in one place so you can track the money moving in and out of your life. The info is password-protected so you can keep your accounts private.

DOLLARS AND SENSE: *Mint.com* gives you an instant snapshot of your financial situation, including checking, savings, and credit-card balances; investments; brokerage accounts; mortgages; and 401k plans. The app also tracks and updates your monthly budget so you know when it's okay to go on a shopping spree and when you have to tighten your belt.

Security Guards

In these times of hackers and phishers, giving your financial account information to anybody other than the teller on the other side of a bank window may strike you as insane. If so, your bank's own mobile app (sidebar, next page) may be a better choice than Pageonce or Mint.com. However, for those who want all their accounts in one place, there *are* some reassuring practices in place at both these sites. For one, they use military-level security to encrypt your data. Second, both apps are read-only, meaning they only *display* your current balances—you can't move money in or out of the accounts. Third, if you lose your iPhone or iPod, both services let you go to their website and block access to financial info from the app. Still worried? Set up a passcode lock in your device's Settings area.

Best App for Mobile Banking

USAA Mobile

Free
Version 2.3.1 | USAA
For all iPhones and the iPod Touch

USAA started off as a financial services company for military members, but it expanded its offerings to civilians and now serves 7.4 million people. It's one of the most versatile apps around for managing accounts. You need a USAA membership (available to servicepeople and their families) for *all* of USAA's offerings, like auto and home insurance, but civilians can get and track USAA bank accounts, credit cards, and investments.

POCKET TELLER: USAA Mobile's home screen gives you an overview of your USAA accounts and services. You can see the balances for your financial accounts, payment due dates, and information for any credit-card or insurance coverage you have through USAA. Full USAA members can deposit paper checks by snapping a photo of the endorsed document.

POLICY WONK: If you qualify for auto and home insurance through USAA, the app lets you see the details of your coverage, make payments, and see what's covered. For the auto-insured, the app displays the drivers listed on your policy along with their driver's license numbers. Within the app, you can get quotes for adding or replacing vehicles on the policy.

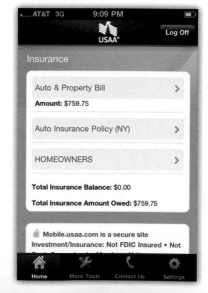

At Home

TIMES OF NEED: True to its roots as a car insurance company, USAA's Auto Incident Assistance is full of helpful tools in your time of need. Along with advice on handling accidents, the app lets you quickly call for roadside assistance should your car break down. Scroll down the list to see the clever flashlight app USAA has thoughtfully included for the dark times.

FULL SERVICE: Tap the More Tools button to get to USAA Mobile's mini-apps for finding an ATM, figuring out a mortgage payment, or trading a stock. You can also do some car searching and shopping here, and if you need to update the copy of your current car's insurance card, tap away to have USAA Auto email you a ready-to-print PDF.

Bank on It

If you're not a USAA member or don't use any of the company's financial services, you can probably find an app for your own bank. Just about every major financial institution has climbed onboard the mobile-banking train, so pop into the App Store and type *banking* into the search box. Chase, Bank of America, SunTrust, PNC, Wells Fargo, and Citi are just a few of the big names that have their own apps for managing accounts and bank-issued credit cards. The apps themselves are free, but you need an online account to log in. (Stop by your local branch and have a customer-service representative help you if you don't have a user name and password.) For even more accounts to manage, some credit-card companies, like American Express and Discover Card, also have their own apps in the Store now.

Best App for Sticking to Your Budget

Ace Budget
Free | $0.99 for full version
Version 3.7.7 | Steve Tran
For all iPhones and the iPod Touch

Pinching pennies is nobody's idea of a good time (well, *almost* nobody's), but Ace Budget adds some color to the tedious task. Use the app to create budgets for various cycles (daily, weekly, monthly, and so on) and then record your expenses to keep yourself on track. You can schedule financial-transaction deductions (and set up alerts for them), too. If you're trying to save money on apps, the Lite version is free—but limits you to 20 transactions.

At Home

RUNNING TALLY: Setting up a budget is simple. Record how much money comes into your house every month (from salaries and other personal income), then set limits for what you want to spend on regular expenses. Each time you make a purchase, tap it into the app under the proper category to see how much of your allowance is left.

PIECES OF THE PIE: To get a visual breakdown of your budget, tap the Reports button to see a pie-chart version of your household finances. You can see charts showing expenses versus income, expenses by budget, and income by budget. Tap the arrows near the top of the screen to see the chart for the previous or next budget cycle.

Best App for Trading Stocks

E*Trade Mobile Pro
Free
Version 1.7 | Etrade Financial
For all iPhones and the iPod Touch

Serious investors, casual day traders, and people who just want to see what the stock market is doing to their 401k accounts will like E*Trade's wonderful app. When logged in, account holders can place market and limit orders, set alerts, and get real-time quotes. Even non-E*Traders can access financial news and market commentary. Alas, the E*Trade baby does not pop up to provide video stock quotes.

STOCK IN TRADE: E*Trade Mobile Pro lets you research companies you may want to invest in to see their current share price as well as their 52-week high and low prices. Tap the Get Quotes button to enter a company's ticker symbol (or to look up the ticker symbol). Flick down the screen to read recent news stories from BusinessWire and *MarketWatch.com*.

 HONORABLE MENTION

iStockManager
Free
Version 2.2.1 | iStockManager LLC
For all iPhones and the iPod Touch

If you like to keep an eye on what moves markets, TD Ameritrade's iStockManager is an informative app for those with or without a TD Ameritrade account. It displays market news from Midnight Trader, Yahoo, and Google News to keep you informed. Anyone can enter stock ticker symbols to watch quotes (non-member quotes may be delayed by up to 20 minutes), and TD Ameritrade account holders can buy and sell shares, too.

Best App for Home-Loan Calculations

Mortgage Calc Pro
$1.99
Version 1.2 | Eamonn and Ian LLC
For all iPhones and the iPod Touch

The thrill of buying a new house is often dampened by trying to figure out what kind of mortgage you can afford. If you find yourself stymied, consider Mortgage Calc Pro. It figures the total costs and payments for both fixed and adjustable-rate mortgages, and its built-in glossary sheds light on terms like "marginal tax rate" and "PMI." And it's not just a one-time app either—its refinancing calculator can be helpful a few years later.

LOAN SHARK: To jump in with Mortgage Calc Pro, you need to tell it what type of loan you're considering. The app can run the numbers on 15- and 30-year fixed-rate loans, adjustable-rate mortgages in different term lengths, interest-only ARM loans, and loans lasting anywhere from 1 to 360 months. Tap the Email Summary button to transfer the info to a message.

HOUSING COSTS: The amount of money you need to borrow is just one of the many costs associated with buying a home. The app includes a worksheet to punch in the digits for all those other things you have to pay for at closing time, like points you're carrying on the loan, homeowner's insurance premiums, real-estate taxes, and so on.

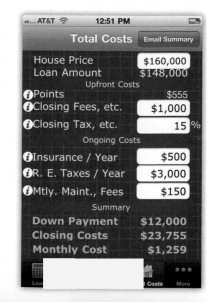

At Home

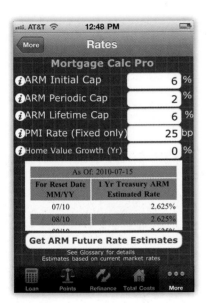

CalcsPro Mortgage Calculator

Free | $1.99 for full version
Version 1.42.2 | Mortal Geek LLC
For all iPhones and the iPod Touch

If you're going for a fixed-rate loan and want to know the overall cost, consider the CalcsPro Mortgage Calculator. Not quite as versatile (or as easy to read) as Mortgage Calc Pro, it still quickly crunches the numbers as you shop for a loan. The ad-supported freebie edition, Calcs-Free, doesn't offer detailed analysis or advice like CalcsPro does, but it still does the heavy lifting and factors in your estimated tax savings on a loan.

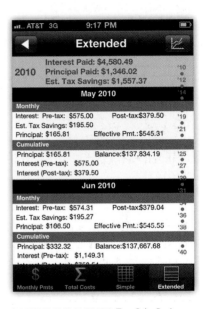

ARM AND LEGWORK: Adjustable-rate mortgages (where interest rates vary over the length of your loan) are harder to calculate than the more predictable fixed-rate loans (where the monthly payment is the same for the life of the loan). To get a sense of what you'll be paying, tap the More button, choose Rates, and type in the ARM info you get from your lender.

BACK TO THE FUTURE: Tap CalcsPro's Simple button to see a basic table showing the interest, principle, and balance you'll pay over the life of your loan. Tap the Extended button to see the total cost of the loan, broken down into even smaller data nuggets, like cumulative pre- and post-tax interest. Tap the icon on the upper-right to see all of it graphed out.

Best App for Entertaining Toddlers

Hippo Hooray Colors

$0.99
Version 3.1 | Jackson Fish Market LLC
For all iPhones and the iPod Touch

Most toddlers are magically drawn to LCD screens (usually after eating jelly sandwiches). Hippo Hooray Colors gives them a preschool workout when they grab for your iPhone or Touch. The app uses touch-sensitive flash cards to teach your little one colors. Select the right-hued cupcake, leaf, or other shape, and Junior gets lauded (occasionally by a pop-up video); pick the wrong color and he gets help.

SIMPLE RULES: Hippo Hooray Colors teaches your fidgety one colors in two ways: It presents a set of screens that either ask him to touch a certain color, or to pick out the item that's a different color from the rest. Your bairn doesn't have to read because a youthful voice explains the challenge—and helps the tyke until he gets it right.

POSITIVE REINFORCEMENT: When your child taps the correct color, the app responds with current-day forms of praise, like "Awesome!" or "Super cool!" or "You rock!" (Parents may want to put on headphones after a few rounds of the game.) When your child completes a series of flash cards, the app displays animated fireworks or a cheer from the eponymous hippo.

touch orange

HOORAY!

Best App for Being "The Cat in the Hat"

Dr. Seuss Camera
$1.99
Version 1.2 | Oceanhouse Media Inc.
For all iPhones and the iPod Touch

With some help from your iPhone's camera, the Dr. Seuss Camera app lets kids put themselves (or whomever else is around) into one of the most popular children's books of all time. (Camera-less Touch owners can import pictures synced from iTunes or saved from mail messages.) Once your child combines Seuss with self in one of the provided scenes, she can save the results to your gadget's photo library.

PICTURE THIS: Dr. Seuss Camera offers 16 cards with scenes and characters from *The Cat in the Hat*. The drawings, based on Seuss's original artwork, include cutouts for photos. Swipe the screen to cycle through the cards; tap one to pick it. After you take a photo (or import an existing one), you can add colorful borders and stamps to personalize the card before saving it.

FRAME SHOP: With you aiming the camera, your child's face can appear right under the familiar feline's candy-striped top hat. Other photo templates require less precision. Once you have a photo in place, the app lets you move and resize it to get just the right look. When you finish, you can save the pic or email it to a grandparent or best friend.

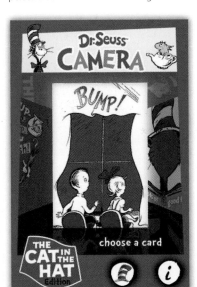

Best App for Early Education

Teach Me: Kindergarten
$0.99
Version 2.1.1 | 24x7digital LLC
For all iPhones and the iPod Touch

The young'uns can learn spelling, word recognition, and basic arithmetic from the TeachMe: Kindergarten app. A cartoon teacher, Mimi Mouse, guides kids through the app's lessons with audio instructions, but it's not a hands-off program. You can adjust Teach Me's settings to focus on certain subjects and then check your child's progress with an on-screen report card.

LETTER-PERFECT: Kids learn basic spelling and word-recognition by dragging a missing letter from the bottom of the screen to the appropriate position within a word. Mimi Mouse, in the top-right corner, offers instruction and encouragement as your offspring works her way through word and math puzzles that become increasingly more challenging.

REWARD POSTERS: When it comes to motivating kids to learn, nothing works like bribery. When a child answers three questions correctly, Mimi Mouse gives her a gold coin as incentive to keep going. Your sprout can redeem the coins for virtual stickers, and add her loot to a tiny digital poster. She can also save the sticker collection as wallpaper or email it to friends.

Best App for Digital Picture Books

iReading Animation Stories

$2.99
Version 1.0 | Max Stage Technology
For all iPhones and the iPod Touch

Children typically learn to read by being read *to*, and iReading Animation Stories includes six digital-picture books with lively images and audio narration. It's not a lightweight app—you need 150MB of space to add it to your gadget—but the half-dozen tales will keep young readers occupied through at least one dinner course, and teach them to read at the same time.

TALKING PICTURES: Each illustrated audiobook includes a short animated "story movie" that flashes the character's dialogue on-screen. The word-learning section (below) repeats some of the movie's lines on-screen to help kids learn to read.

READ ME: Kids can read a line for themselves or tap the word balloon to hear it read to them. To turn the "pages," tap the question-mark bubbles at the bottom of the screen. Tap the arrow in the top-left corner to return to the app's main menu.

Best App for Drawing Little Pictures

Doodle Buddy
Free | $0.99 for full version
Version 1.21 | Pinger Inc.
For all iPhones and the iPod Touch

If you can't drag a box of 64-color Crayolas and a drawing tablet with you on a trip, whip out Doodle Buddy instead. The app, which has 44,000 colors, lets kids (and adults) paint and draw pictures on the screen and then add virtual stamps and stickers to their squiggles. Two or more Doodle Buddy users can draw together. The Premium version of the app adds more stamps and subtracts the advertising.

FINGER PAINT: In addition to drawing on an empty canvas, Doodle Buddy lets you apply your skills to photo backgrounds. To start over with a blank slate, give the iPhone or iPod Touch a gentle shake (just like Etch-a-Sketch!). Save memorable works to the app's photo album, email them to relatives and buddies you add to the app's Friends list, or post them to Facebook.

ARTIST'S PALETTE: Tap the brush icon in the bottom row to change the drawing tool you're using (paintbrush or chalk), or to "smudge" the pixels. Move the slider down at the bottom of the screen to adjust the thickness of the line you draw. You can wipe out portions of a drawing with the Eraser tool. Tap the rubber stamp icon to add stickers to your work.

Best App for Young Zoologists

Baby Animals Encyclopedia Game

Free | $0.99 for full version
Version 1.1 | Adelante Consulting Inc.
For all iPhones and the iPod Touch

From just-born zoo critters to pint-size Disney varmints, young animals fascinate young humans. The Baby Animals Encyclopedia Game uses that connection to teach kids about the natural world. The crisp, clear photos of 90 babies (the paid version includes more) make it a wonderful app to browse, and kids can see that everyone has someone around them who's bigger than they are.

PHOTO ID: Baby Animals' Photo Quiz shows kids four baby animals and asks them to pick the one named on the screen. Correct answers are often greeted with a Homer Simpson-like "Woo hoo!", while misses generate a befuddled "Huh?" The similar Name Quiz shows just one animal and three names to pick from.

FACT BOOK: The app includes more than pictures. When you see an animal you like, tap the Info button to flip the picture around like a baseball card so you can read a detailed description of the creature. If you like a particular photo, shake your iPhone or Touch to save the image to the device's photo album.

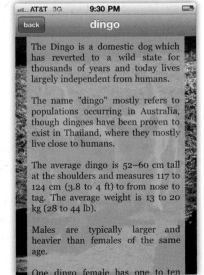

Best App for Learning the Numbers

KidCalc 7-in-1 Math Fun

$0.99
Version 1.12.3 | Steve Glinberg
For all iPhones and the iPod Touch

KidCalc 7-in-1 Math Fun's interactive flash cards and engaging puzzles give preschoolers and kindergartners a grounding in simple math as it entertains them. For the older set (elementary-school children), the app covers more advanced arithmetic lessons, including multiplication and division as well as addition and subtraction. It also teaches them how to count up to 1,000.

REVEALING ANSWERS: KidCalc's Math Puzzle presents a quartet of arithmetic problems. For each correct answer, a colored tile falls away to reveal a hidden picture. The app keeps things lively by animating problems with objects like basketballs and stars to illustrate the numeric amounts involved. Tap the picture-frame icon to change the color of the tiles.

TRACE EFFECTS: KidCalc gives children practice writing out numbers —no pencil and paper needed. As the child traces the number with a finger, KidCalc fills in the outline and announces the name of the number. Tap the ↻ icon to see the app flip around the numeral and display the same number represented by items like party hats.

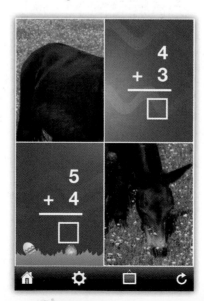

At Home

SOUND CHOICES: KidCalc Math lets you change the voice used in the games' audio prompts. Other settings let you turn the sound off completely (handy for public venues like airplanes). You can also have the program announce numbers as they appear on-screen, or have it wait until the child touches the screen before the audio kicks in.

MATH MACHINE: Kids get their own basic calculator for free-form addition and subtraction. As a tot taps in each number, the corresponding number of objects appear to reinforce the concept of quantity. Unlike those boring old Texas Instruments models, you can gussy up this calculator in several colors and themes by tapping the picture-frame icon.

WINTER GAMES: A winter-themed game has your child tap the screen to count a certain number of snowflakes falling gently over a cozy cabin illuminated by a brightly lit pine tree. To add a bit of cheer to the tranquility of the animated flakes, the app offers music-box renditions of two popular Christmas tunes and one all-purpose joyful Hebrew folk song.

Best App for DIY To-Do Lists

DIY List
$0.99
Version 1.0 | Hurryforward Ltd.
For all iPhones and the iPod Touch

Getting organized is one of the first steps in any do-it-yourself project, and DIY List has you covered. It gives you detailed item lists for more than a dozen jobs. You can create multiple lists, too, so you can handle several tasks at once (yeah, right). A peek at a list quickly tells you what you still need to do, but you don't have to open the app to see how many tasks are left for your top project—the app icon on your iPhone's home screen tells you.

CATEGORICAL IMPROVEMENTS: You won't have a problem finding to-do lists in the App Store, but DIY List comes stocked with categories and lists specifically for do-it-yourself projects and chores. Tap a category to see a list of common items, then tap any item you want to add to your to-do list. You can annotate stock items and add your own.

RED CROSS: One of the best things about lists is marking off completed tasks. You do that here by just tapping the item. An animated red pencil slash appears over the finished chore. When you mark off the last item on your list, the words "You've finished" appear on-screen. If you have recurring lists or need a mulligan, tap Start Over at the bottom of the screen.

Best App for Buying Materials

DIY Calculator
$0.99
Version 1.2 | CleverMatrix Ltd.
For all iPhones and the iPod Touch

Knowing *what* to buy for DIY jobs is one thing, but knowing *how much* of it to buy is another matter, especially for major projects. Fortunately, DIY Calculator does the math for you. It figures out how many gallons of paint you need to cover the ceiling or how much wallpaper to buy for that bathroom renovation. The numbers are estimates, but they get you in the ballpark so you don't buy too much or too little.

MEASURED ANSWERS: To calculate how much raw material you need, tap the item you're shopping for—paint, wallpaper, flooring, or tile—and enter the dimensions of the room. (Be sure to tap the proper units of measure, like gallons, too.) For wall coverings like paint and wallpaper, the app includes sliders to account for windows and doors.

AREAS OF COVERAGE: DIY Calculator automatically factors in seam-matching and broken pieces when it determines how much wallpaper or tile you need for a room. When you get your estimate, you can email it (perhaps to a spouse already at Home Depot) or save it within the app to refer to later, like when you're at the building-supply store.

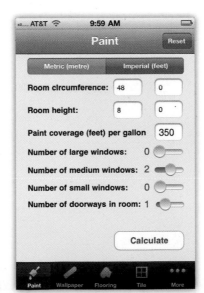

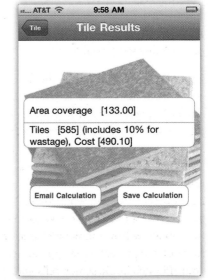

Best App for Virtual Toolbelts

iHandy Carpenter
$1.99
Version 2.0 | iHandySoft Inc.
For all iPhones and the iPod Touch

In an elegant fusion of form and function, iHandy Carpenter includes five tools for the industrious DIYer. You get a ruler for measurements, a protractor for angles, a surface and bubble level to keep you on an even keel, and a gently swinging plumb bob for vertical precision. Beautifully rendered in simulated brushed steel, textured wood, and realistic shadows, iHandy Carpenter looks notably crisp on the iPhone 4's high-res display.

LEVEL UP: Before taking measurements with iHandy Carpenter, calibrate the app by holding your phone or iPod against a flat surface in its vertical, horizontal, and face-up orientations while tapping the on-screen Calibrate button. Tap the ❶ icon to get to the settings for buttons and audio alerts, and for the built-in help guide.

BOBBING WITH APPLES: Of all the tools in iHandy Carpenter's kit, the plumb bob is the most fun to look at, even if you're not actually using it to mark vertical reference lines. As one might expect, the plumb bob only works in portrait mode, while most of the other tools work best in landscape view.

At Home

Best App for Handyman Jargon

Handyman Glossary

$0.99
Version 1.0 | Deep Powder Software
For all iPhones and the iPod Touch

Trade crafts have a language all their own, and if you're just starting to learn the lingo as you shop the local hardware store, this app can save you a lot of Googling when you get home. Handyman Glossary doesn't offer flashy graphics or animation, but if you need a quick, precise explanation of the difference between closed- and open-grain wood or what VERP means, this app is your Rosetta Stone.

SHORT TERMS: If you don't need answers immediately, Handyman Glossary displays its contents in an alphabetized list that's easy to browse. Slide your finger down the vertical row of letters on the right to jump around. Tap an entry to see the full definition of a term; most explanations are one or two sentences long at most.

WORD SEEK: Handyman Glossary includes a search function that scours the app's DIY terms and their definitions for your requested word. It rounds up and displays entries where the word appears. You call up the Search box by tapping the Keyword button at the bottom-left of the app's screen (below left).

Best App for Decorating Ideas

Dream Home
Free | $1.99 for full version
Version 1.2 | MYW Productions
For all iPhones and the iPod Touch

Even if you think you know how you want to redo the living room, take a peek inside other people's homes for more ideas. Dream Home is a pocket-sized look-book for interior design, illustrated with professional photos that show off different spaces (living room, bedroom, and so on). The app's creators add new images regularly, and Dream Home's paid version offers additional photos on a screen uncluttered by ads.

VIEW WITH A ROOM: Dream Home offers several ways to browse for ideas. Tap the buttons in the top row to see pictures of rooms based on color theme or decorating style, like modern or traditional. Tap the Play button in the bottom row and the photos slide by automatically.

PICTURE SHOW: To get an uncluttered view of a room, tap the photo so that it expands to fill the screen. You can use the iPhone and iPod Touch's pinch-and-spread moves to zoom in and out of an image, and you can drag part of a photo to the center of the screen to better see its details.

Best App for Household Management

HomeRoutines

$4.99
Version 1.6 | Wunderbear Software Ltd.
For all iPhones and the iPod Touch

Bringing order out of chaos is a full-time job, especially in a house teeming with family members and pets. Inspired by the FlyLady self-help group for organizing your life, Home-Routines breaks down the task of de-cluttering one's house and life into regular routines. To keep things moving, HomeRoutines includes a built-in timer so you can see just how much you can do in 15 minutes (or whatever amount of time you choose).

HABIT-FORMING: HomeRoutine's pre-loaded tasks give you a start on organizing your day and week, but you can customize everything to reflect your own household. Tap Edit to reorganize tasks in the default routine or to add a new one. Within each routine's list of tasks, you can delete those that don't apply to you (say, if you have no cat to feed).

ZONE DEFENSE: One tenet of the FlyLady way of life is dividing your house into a series of "zones" and concentrating on one zone each week. Every zone has a daily cleaning mission designed to take no longer than 15 minutes, and the chores serve as a preemptive strike against having to spend days doing a massive cleaning all at once.

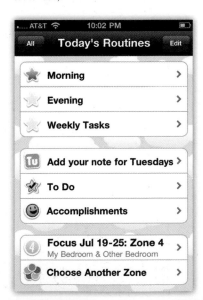

Best Apps On the Road

Travel can be an adventure—in more ways than one. Whether you're heading out on a big family vacation or going solo on a tour of your company's international sales offices, most trips begin long before you hop in a car or board a plane.

If you're looking for a way to keep everything under control, from planning your excursion to remembering it fondly, break out your iPhone or iPod Touch. With the right apps, that shiny little slab becomes your trusty companion throughout your journey.

Once you decide to travel, your iPhone can steer you to the **planes, trains, and automobiles** that'll get you where you're going. You'll find apps that help you book flights, hotels, and rental cars; pack your bags; and track your itinerary, no matter how complex.

When you get where you're going, you can use your iPhone to **see the sights** and share your adventures (and trip details) with the folks back home. Whether you're hitting the highway in the U.S. of A. or roaming around internationally, there's an iPhone app to keep you on track.

And speaking of globe-trotting, the iPhone can preview upcoming locales for multi-city trips as you **explore the world**, and it makes a handy pocket translator for dozens of languages, so you can leave your phrase book at home.

Photo: Daniel Silveira

Best App for Booking Cheap Trips

Kayak
Free | $0.99 for full version
Version 11.3 | Kayak Software Corp.
For all iPhones and the iPod Touch

Don't waste your time booking trips on separate airline sites or travel services like Expedia and Orbitz. Fire up Kayak, type in your trip coordinates, and watch Kayak scour them to find the lowest prices and widest selection of hotel rooms, flights, and rental cars. Book online or by phone with the tap of a key. Kayak's First Class version ditches banner ads on the results pages and scouts for first-and business-class airfares as well.

BOOK 'EM: Tap the appropriate icon in the top row of Kayak's home screen to search out the cheapest beds, plane seats, and wheels for your trip. The next group of buttons lets you check out the amenities at major airports, track your flights, see how much each airline is charging you in tacked-on fees *this* week, and save your itinerary to *Kayak.com*.

PICK A FLIGHT: Once you enter your flight's starting and ending cities, travel dates, and number of passengers, Kayak's search engine revs up and collects flights and fares from across the Web. Tap a flight that suits your needs and budget, and Kayak displays its arrival/departure details, along with tappable phone numbers and website URLs so you can reserve a seat.

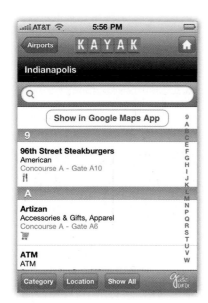

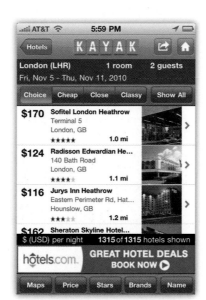

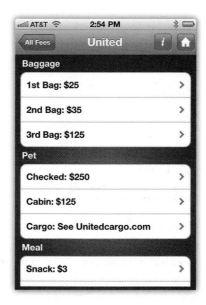

KILL TIME: If you've got a long layover or your flight's been delayed, tap Kayak's Airports icon to see shops, restaurants, bars, and other hangouts where you can while away the hours in the airport you're stuck in—or in the airport you're headed to on the next leg of your journey. Kayak also shows you local ATMs, newsstands, and business centers.

BOOK A BED: Kayak's Hotel search rounds up all the accommodations near you (helpful if your flight gets canceled) or in your destination city. Once you get the results, tap the row of buttons at the top of the screen to see the least expensive, nearest, or fanciest hotel rooms. Tap the buttons below the results to filter by price, star rating, chain, and more.

LAND OF THE FEE: Many airlines, especially domestic carriers, now charge for meals, checked baggage, and even in-flight snacks (a practice called "unbundling"). To see what your airline plans on charging you (besides what they already charged you for your seat), take a breath, tap the Fees icon on the home screen, and find your airline in the list.

Best App for Organizing Your Itinerary

TripDeck
Free
Version 1.5.2 | Mobiata LLC
For all iPhones and the iPod Touch

TripDeck lets you keep all your trip's vital information—confirmation numbers, reservations, meeting times, notes, and so on—in one tidy place. You can easily email your itinerary to family, friends, and colleagues who may need to reach you on the road, or sync your schedule with the TriptIt website to keep a copy online. Although TripDeck itself is free, the app offers extra features, like flight maps and travel alerts, that cost $4 each.

PLAN AHEAD: Staying on top of your airline tickets and confirmation numbers can be hassle enough, but when you factor in the coordinates for hotels, rental cars, business meetings, dinner reservations, train schedules, and the other minutiae of work travel, you'll appreciate TripDeck's organizational skills—it displays all of your info on an easy-to-navigate Quick Reference screen.

SHARE YOUR PLANS: Jam-packed business trips can give you information overload as you try to remember what meeting comes next and where you need to be. Tap an item on the Quick Reference screen (below left) to see just a segment of your journey, neatly isolated on its own screen (below). You can email a copy of that one item—or your entire itinerary—by tapping the envelope button.

Best App for Stuffing Your Suitcase

Packing Pro
$2.99
Version 4.1 | Quinn Genzel
For all iPhones and the iPod Touch

Whether you take an annual vacation with the family or hit the road twice a month on business, Packing Pro makes sure you don't forget anything. Not only does it offer checklists for clothing and toiletries, it reminds you to pack your pills, camcorder, and swim goggles. In addition, its handy pre-trip checklists prompt you to do essential tasks before you leave, like suspending mail delivery and changing your office voicemail.

LISTS OF LISTS: Packing Pro offers a checklist for just about every aspect of a trip, divided into eight categories. The categories themselves have their own subcategories of lists to make sure you don't forget anything. If you tap Toiletries, for example, you'll see that topic divided into lists for hair, face, mouth, and body products.

CUSTOM TAILORING: Once you select a list you want to use—Clothes, for example—you can modify it by adding different types and amounts of gear (depending on the length of your trip and how often you want to change). Tap a line item to enter a new amount and to add information like weight and value in case something goes wrong in the baggage area.

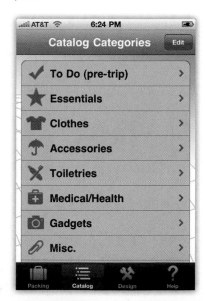

185

Best App for Tracking Flights

Flight Update Pro

$9.99
Version 4.1 | Silverware Software
For all iPhones and the iPod Touch

The App Store is full of great flight-tracking apps—including rival FlightTrack Pro—but Flight Update Pro edges out the competition with bold, colorful graphics and seating charts for many planes, courtesy of *SeatGuru.com*. In addition to displaying the current status of your flight, Flight Update Pro shows you gate and baggage-claim info, the local weather, and layover times. If a flight gets cancelled, you can search for alternates.

UP IN THE AIR: Flight Update Pro's neatly designed status screen makes it easy to see all your flight info, including arrival and departure times and meals available, at just a glance. Tap the Options button to bring up the plane's seating chart, the local weather forecast, and alternate flights. Tap the Send button to fire off a copy of your status by email or SMS message.

MAPPED OUT: Tap Flight Update Pro's Map button to see your plane's position in the sky, plotted on a Google map. Other facts about your flight, like its altitude, speed, and estimated time of arrival, put the plane's progress in perspective. Have the app update the map at set intervals, or tap the Refresh button to do so whenever you want.

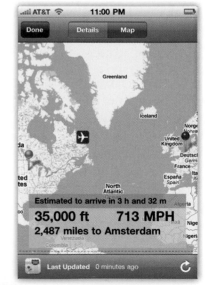

UPDATE YOUR UPDATES: The Prefs button not only lets you set the timer for status updates, it lets you set your preferences for the units of measure you want to use for temperature and wind speed. Like many travel-themed apps, Flight Update Pro works with the free TripIt site so you can store a copy of your itinerary online. You can link to the site from this screen.

FlightTrack Pro
$9.99
Version 3.6.2 | Mobiata LLC
For all iPhones and the iPod Touch

This rival to Flight Update Pro also does a superb job of monitoring and mapping planes in the air—and those still trying to get off the ground. FlightTrack Pro seamlessly integrates with the free TripIt site, so if you send flight confirmation emails to TripIt, the flight shows up in FlightTrack Pro. The app supports the iPhone 4's high-res display, so even maps depicting bad weather look great. Don't have any trips of your own to track? Shake your iPhone to check out a randomly chosen flight.

INFO AT A GLANCE: Add a trip to Flight-Track Pro and you get all sorts of information on the flight, as well as how much time you have to make your connections. The app reveals how late a plane may have pushed away from the departing gate and predicts its appearance at the arriving gate. Tap the airport name to get weather conditions and FAA alerts for that location.

Best App for Stops off the Interstate

iExit
$2.99
Version 2.1 | Allstays LLC
For all iPhones and the iPod Touch

Billboards and blue highway signs list only a fraction of the restaurants, rest stops, gas stations, and other necessities available off of each interstate exit. Fortunately, iExit fills in the gaps, using the iPhone's GPS to pinpoint your location and show you all the eateries, service stations, chain stores, and more available at the nearest exit. If you're not ready to stop just yet, the app shows you what's available an amazing 150 exits down the road.

EYE IN THE SKY: Thanks to the iPhone's GPS, iExit knows when you're on the road and when you're not. It presents you with nearby amenities as you approach each exit. Tap the gear icon to adjust what you see. For example, if you don't care about diesel gas stations or campgrounds, you can turn those off so iExit doesn't waste pixels displaying them.

POINT A TO POINT B: When you *do* find a restaurant, hotel, rest stop, or other establishment worth pulling off the highway for, tap its entry in the Exit list to get more information. The app displays the place's location on a map, provides a phone number you can tap to call it, and even generates directions from the exit ramp, courtesy of Google Maps.

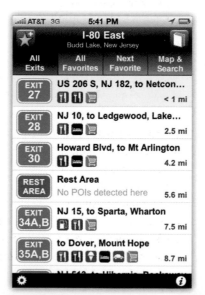
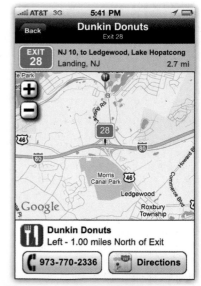

On the Road

EASE ON DOWN THE ROAD: You don't have to wait to get to an exit to see what's available in an upcoming area. You can browse for potential lunch stops for tomorrow's all-day drive the night before (Touch users, do your research using the hotel's Wi-Fi). Tap the book icon to call up iExit's Exit Lookup feature and find out what awaits you at each exit nationwide.

⊕ **HONORABLE MENTION**

AroundMe

Free
Version 4.00 | Tweakersoft
For all iPhones and the iPod Touch

Whether you're in a car or walking around an unfamiliar town, AroundMe uses the iPhone's GPS to display a list of area hotels, restaurants, gas stations, hospitals, pharmacies, banks, ATMs, and other points of interest. To get a different perspective, activate the iPhone's camera and turn the device horizontally. Business names float above the real-life buildings in the app's "augmented reality" mode, a mashup of what the iPhone's camera sees and its compass function.

YOU ARE HERE: AroundMe's breakdown of businesses into sensible categories makes it a great app not only for unfamiliar locales, but for finding stuff right in your home town. When you need to find a gas station to fill up the tank or a nearby supermarket to fill up the cooler for a day's drive, AroundMe shows you what's available in the 'hood.

189

Best App for Hailing a Cab

Rocket Taxi
$1.99
Version 2.5 | Edovia Inc.
For all iPhones and the iPod Touch

To grab a cab just about anywhere in the world, check out Rocket Taxi's list of 27,500 taxi companies in 10,000 cities. The app's database works fine offline, but when you're online, it identifies your location and suggests local cab companies for your conveyance. The app's Trip Calculator estimates the fare as you ride along, and the currency converter tells you what your trip will cost in the coin of the realm.

CAB DOOR TO THE WORLD: Rocket Taxi's extensive listings let you ring up cab companies in thousands of cities around the world with just a tap on the screen. You can review the star ratings to winnow your choices, add preferred companies to your Favorites list, and report outdated information to the app's developers. If you run into a cur of a cabby, rate him by swiping a set of stars.

CASH CONVERSIONS: Rocket Taxi's trip calculator displays a suggested route, gauges the distance between your pickup location and your destination, estimates the fare, and converts it to the local currency so you can tip appropriately. Keep in mind that an estimate is an estimate and may not account for local surcharges or cabbies forgetting to change zone information for your ride.

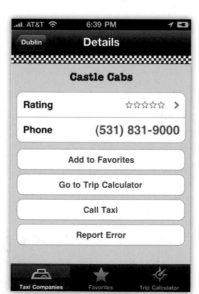

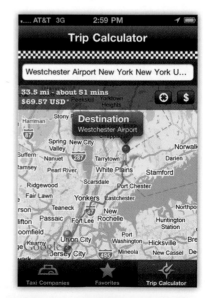

Best App for Navigating Mass Transit

HopStop

Free
Version 1.4 | HopStop.com Inc.
For all iPhones and the iPod Touch

HopStop's iPhone app is a portable version of the popular website that devotes itself to getting you from Point A to Point B by train, bus, taxi, or on foot. HopStop knows the transit systems for most large East Coast cities, as well as for Atlanta, Chicago, London, and Paris. Type in your start and end points, pick a transport method, and hit Go. HopStop plots your route step-by-step and transfer-by-transfer, in both text and on maps.

FINDING YOUR WAY: Getting around unfamiliar cities can be confusing enough on foot, but adding mass transit into the mix can send you around the bend. With HopStop, just type in the addresses you're leaving from and going to, and the app's detailed instructions take all the worry out of changing trains or transferring buses.

STEP BY STEP: Once HopStop analyzes your travel wishes, it presents you with a list of directions on how to get there. Flick to the bottom of the screen to see the prescribed route mapped out. You can email the directions (a great feature if *you're* the local trying to get visiting pals around town) and save routes that you may take again.

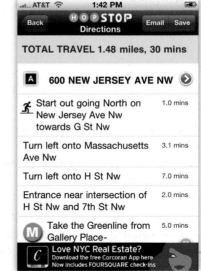

Best App for Visiting Big Cities

MyCityWay Guides
Free to $1.99
Version 3.1 | Srividya Tech Inc.
For all iPhones and the iPod Touch

With 50 to 60 mini-apps bundled into one mega-app, MyCityWay's urban guides put a city's resources in the palm of your hand—literally. You can check local events, tours, hotels, parking lots, Wi-Fi hotspots, shops, and more. A free app is available for New York, San Francisco, London, Seattle, Chicago, Portland, and Los Angeles. Apps for Boston and Washington, DC, cost 99 cents each, and Las Vegas will run you two bucks.

OODLES OF ICONS: Open MyCityWay's icon for your chosen city (see Chicago, that toddlin' town, below) to bring up several screens' worth of additional icons, all dedicated to local listings and information on particular topics, like parking or coffee shops. Tap the 🔍 icon at the top of the screen to search for a business by name if you don't know its category.

NAMES AND NUMBERS: When you find an establishment you'd like to visit, tap MyCityWay's map icon to see just where it is. In addition to marking the spot on a map, MyCityWay lists the address and phone number. Tap the little green phone icon to leave MyCityWay and make the call. Just be mindful of roaming charges if you're overseas.

Best App for Admiring Architecture

Modern Architecture Guide
$1.99
Version 1.10 | MIMOA
For all iPhones and the iPod Touch

If admiring the works of Le Corbusier, Frank Lloyd Wright, or any other major modern architect is your idea of a dream vacation, the Modern Architecture Guide is a worthy travel companion. Stocked with photos, descriptions, and facts for 3,500 buildings, parks, and other locations around the world, the app uses the iPhone's location services to pinpoint nearby treasures.

WONDERS OF THE WORLD: The Modern Architecture guide uses your current location to find buildings of note near you. The Search function lets you look up architectural wonders by name or location. When you find something interesting, tap its listing to see the address and background on the structure. You can also get directions to it.

WHAT YOU SEE: Most of Modern Architecture Guide's entries include photographs of the destination buildings or location so you can decide whether it's worth your time. Some public structures or institutions have their own websites, so the app includes a button that launches Safari and takes you to these dedicated pages for additional reading.

Julie Fuchs

Best App for Oddball Americana

Roadside America

$2.99 for one US region
Version 1.1 | This Exit LLC
For all iPhones and the iPod Touch

Everyone's seen the Liberty Bell and the Grand Canyon, but how many people have seen Delaware's annual pumpkin-catapult contest or the "Nuns of the Battlefield" sculpture in Washington, DC? Roadside America catalogues quirky, offbeat, and just plain fun national attractions for those in search of a unique vacation. The app unlocks one of six US regions (Northeast, Midwest, and so on); an annual $6 gives you the whole country.

TOURIST TRACKS: Once you unlock your chosen region (or pony up the six bucks for the entire nation), you can browse lists of nearby attractions—or search by state and city to plan memorable trips ahead of time. Tap Roadside America's Themes button to see sight listings grouped into catchy categories like "Dinosaurs," "Freaky Hoo-Ha," or "Zombie Army."

AIN'T THAT AMERICA: On the listings screen, when an attraction piques your interest, tap its entry to get more information. The Detail screen gives you a description of the site, its address, and directions for getting there based on your current location. User-submitted photos add to the intrigue. You may find yourself suddenly reaching for the car keys.

On the Road

Best App for Maps

Google Earth
Free
Version 3.0 | Google Inc.
For all iPhones and the iPod Touch

For the sheer thrill of swooping in on any city across the globe in animated high-resolution glory, nothing beats Google Earth (on your iPhone *or* your desktop). Type in an address and the app "flies" you there, displaying the area using sharp satellite photos and labelling nearby points of interest. With the iPhone's location services turned on, you can tap the Current Location button to pin your whereabouts to a map.

DOWN HERE BELOW: It's not a new app, but Google Earth continues to improve—and impress—with its Superman view of the world and all its attractions. The app combines beautiful photographs with points-of-interest graphics. For example, tap the silverware icon above to see the name of a restaurant, or tap one of the tiny W's to call up relevant Wikipedia articles.

⊕ HONORABLE MENTION

Offline City Maps
$2.99 to $4.99
Version 1.0 | APlus Software
For all iPhones and the iPod Touch

Google may give you the Earth, but it needs a network connection to do its thing. If you're on a trip without access to the Internet, plan ahead with one of Offline City Maps' 350 maps. In addition to displaying a zoomable street grid for your chosen city, you'll find hundreds of clearly labelled points of interest and thumbnail profiles of each city, which include background info on the burg's size, population, history, and more.

Best App for Globe-Trotting

Fizz Traveller

$5.99
Version 1.1 | Fizz Software Ltd.
For all iPhones and the iPod Touch

"What will the weather be like in Paris tomorrow and in Berlin the day after that?" Jumping time zones and continents can test even the most hardened road warrior, but Fizz Traveller lets you store info for several cities at once, showing you the 5-day forecast, airport conditions, local times, and more for each stop on your trip. The app also includes currency, meeting-time, and clothing-size conversion tools.

WEATHER EVERYWHERE: Once you add all the cities on your journey to Fizz Traveller, you can see what's ahead in each location with a swipe of your finger. The buttons along the bottom of the screen show you 2-day and 5-day forecasts, the current weather conditions for each town, animated maps, and even the weather at airports in the selected cities.

MEASURED CONVERSIONS: One of Fizz Traveller's especially helpful tools is Conversions. It not only converts currency, but measurements for weight, length, temperature, and other standards that vary around the world. And if international differences in wardrobe sizes have stopped you from buying pants and shoes in other countries, try the clothing-size converter.

On the Road

Best App for Speaking in Tongues

Lingopal 44

$1.99 | $9.99 for full version
Version 1.2.2 | Lingopal Holdings Pty. Ltd.
For all iPhones and the iPod Touch

Backpacking through Europe? Lingopal 44 gives you text and audio translations of common phrases (including pick-up lines) in 44 languages, from Afrikaans to Vietnamese. If you don't need all 44 languages at once, you can buy them individually for 99 cents each. Lingopal's free Lite apps, available for many languages (including English), offer only two categories of conversation, for the basics and flirting, but that may be all you need.

WHAT LANGUAGE, PLEASE? When you first fire up LingoPal 44, you see its entire list of available languages. Tap one to select your native tongue (which, by the way, can be any of the languages Lingopal offers) and then select the language you wish to converse in. Then pick your gender to avoid awkward moments with languages that differentiate.

TOPICS OF CONVERSATION: Tap the Categories button to see Lingopal's range of topics and related phrases. The app covers just about all the standard traveler sayings, and a few you may not have thought of. You can add the lines you find most useful to a Favorites list so you don't have to fumble around in Categories to utter an often-used phrase.

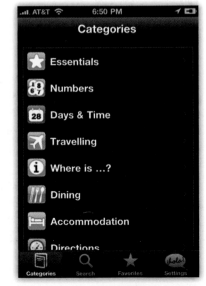

Best App for Blending In

World Customs and Cultures
Free
Version 2.1 | Hooked in Motion LLC
For all iPhones and the iPod Touch

Need to know if making direct eye contact with someone in Japan is socially acceptable, or what gender issues might await you on that business trip to Oman? This free app offers a thumbnail view of the social practices and mores of more than 165 countries. It covers several topics, including greetings, personal space and touching, cultural taboos, and even the local drinking age.

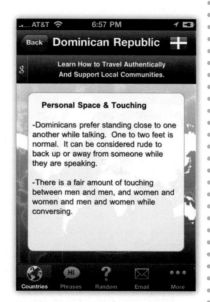

WHEN IN ROME: While it's not as definitive as a diplomat's dossier on local culture and accepted public behavior, World Customs and Cultures offers a thumbnail sketch of what to expect when you travel abroad, especially in countries where the Western world is considered a bit loopy and out of touch with residents in the region.

World Factbook
$0.99
Version 1.2 | Real Puppy Software
For all iPhones and the iPod Touch

Sure to please kids who grew up looking at pictures of international flags tucked into the World Almanac, the World Factbook app does flags and much more. Compiled from information in the CIA World Fact Book, the app provides short histories of countries around the globe. In addition, you'll find details on each nation's current population, geographic coordinates, economy, government, communications, transportation, and military.

Best App for Sharing Adventures

My Vacation

Free | $2.99 for full version
Version 2.0 | Jasper Apps Ltd.
For all iPhones and the iPod Touch

Don't want to haul around a pen and roll of postage stamps on your trip? With the full version of My Vacation, you can turn your own tourist snaps into digital postcards—select a photo, tap out a quick message, and fire it off to all your pals back home to give them a peek at your journey. Both the Lite and Full versions let you record a travel journal with text, audio, and maps to help you remember the good times.

DEAR DIARY: There's no better way to remember a vacation than to keep a travel diary while you're still on it. My Vacation lets you save photos (for Touch users, import them), record audio and video, and write notes about each day's activities. The app also offers local information—tap a city name to get links to maps, weather, and area attractions.

SEND A POSTCARD: Once you add photos to your vacation file, you can turn your favorite snaps into tree-friendly digital postcards. Select a photo and tap the ☛ button to send the picture as an email attachment or a Twitter update. Tap Send Postcard and your photo drops into a template where you can write a note and mail it electronically.

Best Apps
For Your Health

Your iPhone or iPod Touch is more than a communications device or pocket jukebox. Inside that smooth exterior is a tiny computer, one that can store a huge number of personal records, calculate how many sit-ups you need to do to burn off last night's Ben & Jerry's binge, and help you exercise regularly. This chapter shows you how to find apps that let you do all that *and* find your way out of the cold, dark woods.

With rising costs and complications, healthcare has become a major concern for many people. If you have **medical matters** on your mind, you can store your healthcare records electronically and find accurate medical information with several apps. If you see diet, exercise, and eating right as the path to **fitness**, check out apps that track your well-being.

If you're already an active type who'd rather hike across Australia or bike up the side of a mountain, there's a pocketful of programs designed for **the sporting life** and enjoying **the great outdoors**, from quietly planning a backyard garden and listening to the birds to extreme camping. So check the weather, grab your gear, and turn the page for apps that help you reach for the stars.

For Your Health

Best apps for your body & mind

download 'em all

Photo: Thomas Hawk/thomashawk.com

Best App for Healthcare Records

My Medical
$1.99
Version 1.7 | Steven Chaitoff
For all iPhones and the iPod Touch

When it comes to recording your medical history, My Medical puts matters into your own hands. It stores your doctors' contact info, upcoming appointments, lab test results, operations you've had, allergies, prescription medications, emergency contacts, and more in this password-protected pocket database. My Medical is especially handy if you visit a new doctor—you can email him or her your medical history right from the app.

PERMANENT RECORDS: Keep a comprehensive record of your—and your kids'—medical history with My Medical's huge collection of fill-in forms. You can list prescriptions, test results, medical procedures, immunizations, allergies, and more. The first time out, save yourself some tiny-keyboard typing and go to My Medical's website to fill in the forms and send the info to your app.

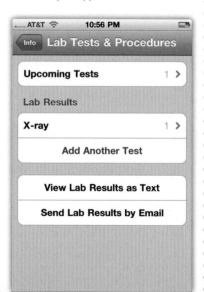

⊕ **HONORABLE MENTION**

WebMD Mobile
Free
Version: 2.0 | WebMD Health Corp.
For all iPhones and the iPod Touch

Need other healthcare info, like translating symptoms into tentative diagnoses, descriptions of health conditions (asthma, diabetes, muscle strain), and information about prescription and over-the-counter drugs? Then WebMD Mobile is a worthy app to have in hand. This iPhone version of the popular online medical reference site includes a first-aid guide and displays nearby general practitioners, specialists, hospitals, and pharmacies on a map.

For Your Health

Best App for Prescription Reference

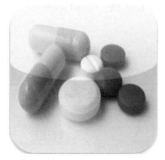

iPharmacy
$0.99 | $1.99 for full version
Version 2.4 | SigmaPhone LLC
For all iPhones and the iPod Touch

Intended as a physician's reference, iPharmacy contains official Food and Drug Administration profiles of more than 7,000 prescription drugs, including information on indications and usage, dosage, adverse reactions, and interactions with other drugs. As you might expect from the name, the $1.99 iPharmacy Professional comes with additional resources for doctors and pharmacists, such as news stories and articles from clinical journals.

DRUG DATA: When your doctor prescribes a drug, iPharmacy can give you detailed information on it, like the symptoms it treats, its effects on your body, and warning signs in case you're allergic. The app includes a PDF of the drug info sheet.

KNOWLEDGE IS POWER: Each drug includes a Dosage & Administration section so you can see the standard dose and dosage range of your medication, recommendations on how often you should be taking it, and recommended maximum dosages.

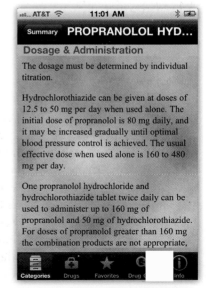

Best App for Dieting and Weight Loss

Tap & Track
$3.99
Version 4.9.5 | Nanobit d.o.o.
For all iPhones and the iPod Touch

If you're a "show me" type who also wants to lose weight, Tap & Track is for you. It records how many calories you consume, how many you burn, and just how many are in that fast-food burrito. Pick a diet plan (lose from ½ to 2 lbs. per week) and Tap & Track logs your meals, exercise, and caloric intake as you work toward your goal. The app's calorie database works offline, so Touch owners can check the counts while eating out, too.

LOG ROLLS: Getting serious about eating better, losing weight, and living a more healthy lifestyle is a big commitment for many people. Tap & Track includes tools to help you plot a plan of action. To achieve balance, the app includes logs that record the number of calories coming in (the Food Log) as well as those going out (the Exercise Log).

PERSONAL FILE: When the holiday eating season ends and you decide to lose those newly acquired 10 pounds, Tap & Track helps you set up a plan of attack. Enter your current weight and the weight you want to be—and stay at. The app tells you how many calories you can consume per day and when you'll reach your goal weight.

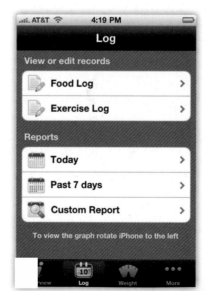

CALORIE COUNTER: Enter everything you eat and every exercise you perform in the battle of the bulge into Tap & Track. The app records your daily stats so you can see how well (or how badly) you're doing. Tap the Full Nutrition Info button to see a snapshot of the day's intake, broken down into total fat, fiber, protein, carbohydrates, sodium, and sugars.

GETTING EXERCISED: Want to know how many calories came off while you were on the rowing machine this morning? Tap & Track includes caloric burn for more than 180 exercises. Dial in the type of activity you engaged in and the amount of time you spent on it to get a rough estimate of the number of calories you burned. The app also has a Body Mass Index calculator.

ROAD FOOD: It's easier to keep track of your calories when you cook your own food and you know what goes into it, but not everyone can eat at home for every meal. Tap & Track includes nutritional information on more than 2,000 brand-name foods and common menu items from more than 700 chain restaurants so you can factor them into your daily food log.

Best App for Personal Training

GymGoal

$0. 99 | $3.99 for full version
Version 5.4.0 | SmalTek
For all iPhones and the iPod Touch

New to fitness training and daunted by exercise machines that look like medieval torture devices? GymGoal shows you what to do—literally. It demonstrates 280 exercises using illustrations and animations and suggests 52 strength-training routines. The app's full version lets you schedule and record daily exercise sessions, and charts your workout history so you can see your progress. You can email workout logs from the app, too.

GYM DANDY: Far cheaper than most personal trainers, GymGoal whips up daily routines based on the equipment you have (like free weights) and the level of difficulty you choose. Make your sessions go faster with GymGoal's built-in MP3 player's free songs or supply your own iPhone or iPod tunes. GymGoal's full version lets you track weights and reps over time.

FLEX TIME: Tap a body part on GymGoal's Body Map to get a list of exercises that enhance just that area. The app gives you on-screen, step-by-step instructions for recommended exercises ("bicycle crunches" or "Russian twists," for example) and demonstrates them with short animated videos so you can be sure you're doing them correctly.

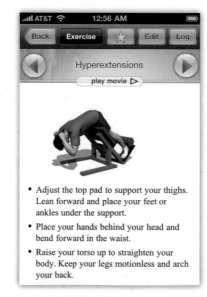

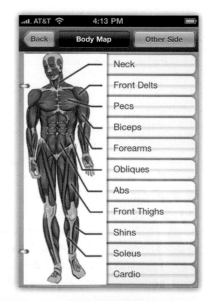

206

Best App for Striking a Blissful Pose

Authentic Yoga

$1.99
Version 1.6 | Signal Patterns
For all iPhones and the iPod Touch

Yoga devotees Deepak Chopra and Tara Stiles teamed up to create this on-the-go yoga experience for the small screen. Authentic Yoga gives you a pocket full of poses that range in difficulty from sheer beginner to advanced yogi, all focused on breathing, body awareness, balance, flexibility, and strength. The app demonstrates the poses in both still and moving pictures, but you need a network connection for video playback.

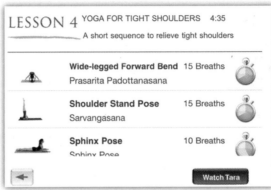

LESSON 4 YOGA FOR TIGHT SHOULDERS   4:35

A short sequence to relieve tight shoulders

Wide-legged Forward Bend 15 Breaths
Prasarita Padottanasana

Shoulder Stand Pose 15 Breaths
Sarvangasana

Sphinx Pose 10 Breaths
Sphinx Pose

Watch Tara

BREATHE DEEP:
Back in your hotel room after a long day sitting in the conference hall? Many of Authentic Yoga's routines help relax certain parts of your body and take just 20 minutes or so. You don't get a yoga mat with the app, so pack your own.

AUDIO-VISUAL AIDS:
When you need a particular pose explained, the app downloads audio files (narrated by Deepak Chopra) and plays back short instructional video clips of yoga teacher Tara Stiles demonstrating the pose or position for you.

Best App for Running

RunKeeper

Free | $9.99 for full verison
Version 2.3.0.2 | RunKeeper LLC
For iPhone 3G, 3GS, and 4

Harnessing the power of the iPhone's GPS chip, RunKeeper tracks your daily runs according to several measures: the distance you ran, your average speed, and the calories you burned. And, thanks to those satellites in the sky, RunKeeper maps your course as you run. The app automatically syncs your stats to the RunKeeper website, where you can track totals and overall progress, and graph your performance over time.

TRACKING TIME: From the moment you take your first step, RunKeeper records your progress on a big, easy-to-read display. It sends each session's activity to the RunKeeper website, where you can compare current and past performance. You can post your stats on Twitter or Facebook right from the app. And if you need a break mid-run, tap the Pause button.

MAP AND GO: Swipe RunKeeper's Activities screen to switch to RunKeeper's Map view, where you appear as a blue dot moving across the screen. Both the free and paid versions offer map-tracking, but busting out a 10-spot for the Pro version adds a handful of tools for serious athletes, like gauging target pace and creating interval workouts.

Best App for Cycling

Cyclemeter GPS

$4.99
Version 4.0 | Abvio LLC
For iPhone 3G, 3GS, and 4

Fire up this GPS stopwatch and hop on your bike. As you pedal over road and trail, Cyclemeter records your speed, location, elevation, time, and distance traveled. You can configure the app to pipe up with audio updates on your time, distance, or new performance records. Cyclemeter pours your accumulated data into graphs and maps so you can track your progress—and beat all of your previous records.

DISTANCE LEARNING: Cyclemeter's Stopwatch uses the iPhone's GPS to calculate speed and distance as you pedal. It displays a screen full of current and averaged statistics, and stores historic data so you can graph and compare your performance over time. You can use Cyclemeter for other activities, too, like hiking, running, and swimming (but consider a waterproof iPhone case if you take to the water).

MAPPING THE ROUTE: Thanks to Cyclemeter's Maps function, you can see where your ride took you and save the route if you want to pass that way again. You can even email the route's Google Map URL to cycling friends. In addition, Cyclemeter adds your routes to its built-in calendar so you know when you took a trip. It stores all your info locally, so you don't need a WiFi connection to review your stats.

Best App for Golfing

ViewTi Golf 2010

Free | $29.99 for full version
Version 2.55 | ViewTi
For iPhone 3G, 3GS, 4, and the iPod Touch

Along with a shot tracker and electronic scorecard, ViewTi Golf gives duffers 3D aerial views of more than 30,000 golf courses worldwide, so you can plot your stroke strategy long before you tee up. The ad-supported free version lets you zoom in and pan around each hole. The paid version includes advanced features like a handicap calculator, the slope reading for each green, and shot analysis using video you take with your iPhone.

COURSE OF ACTION: If you're in the mood for a round of 9 or 18 holes but don't know where to go, ViewTi Golf identifies the courses near you (or you can use the Search box to look for a specific course). Tap a course name to see tee box information. Once you pick your starting tee, ViewTi Golf tracks your shots and keeps score.

TEE TO GREEN: ViewTi Golf displays an aerial view of each hole on a course. It shows you the hole number and par information in the top-left; the number in the middle shows the distance to the center of the green. Tap the red-dotted golf ball icon to activate the program's Shot Tracker, which records your club selection and results for each stroke.

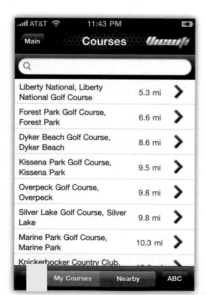

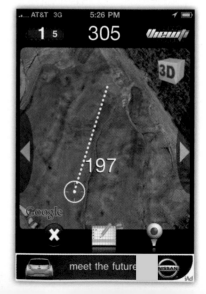

For Your Health

⊕ HONORABLE MENTION

Golf Like a Tour Pro

Free | $4.99 for full version
Version 1.3 | S Squared Golf
For all iPhones and the iPod Touch

The pro in question here is Kevin Streelman, who has appeared on the PGA Tour. The free version of Golf Like a Tour Pro includes shot analysis, tips, and video demonstations from Streelman. The paid version serves as a budget swing coach, with instructions on how to hit 50 kinds of shots from all over the links, along with slow-motion videos that demonstrate just how to get that little white ball to the middle of that vast green green.

FLYOVER COUNTRY: To see the challenge before you as you shoot for the green, tap the 3D button (shown on the previous page) to zoom up to the sky for a perspective view (above) from tee to green, including traps and hazards. Tap the icon on the top-left to replay the flyover, or tap the icon on the right to return to the shot-from-above aerial view.

KEEPING SCORE: Forget about those tiny pencils and crumpled scorecards of yesteryear. Both editions of ViewTi Golf 2010 let you dial in your fairway and green strokes for each hole. To call up the electronic scorekeeper, tap the Scorecard icon (shown on the previous page). If you're shooting a round with friends, the app records the scores of multiple players.

211

Best App for Hiking

MotionX GPS
Free | $2.99 for full version
Version 12.1 | Fullpower Technologies Inc.
For iPhone 3G, 3GS, and 4

Designed for those who like to take their iPhones everywhere they go, MotionX GPS tracks your moves as you hike (or bike, sail, ski, run, or just geocache around town). Once you save a trek, you can view it on a map, share it with friends, or view photos you took along the way (you can snap pics right from the app). The free version allots you just one trip and three waypoints, while the paid app gives you more of both.

TAKE A HIKE: MotionX's menu screen serves as the dashboard for all your global-positioning needs. Tap the My Position button to get a fix on your current location in longitude and latitude; the Share button lets your Twitter and Facebook friends know where you are. Tap the Track Recorder button to record a trip, and Way-points to set stops along the way. Tap the iPod button to add music to the mix.

MAPPED OUT: When you tap the Map button on MotionX's main menu, the app displays your current position and pins it to a street or satellite map. You can zoom in and out of the map with the iPhone's pinch-and-spread finger moves. You can download and store maps from within the app, and change map types (road, satellite, or hybrid) by tapping the calipers icon in the bottom-left corner.

212

Best App for Extreme Camping

SAS Survival Guide
Free | $6.99 for full version
Version 1.2 | Trellisys.net
For all iPhones and the iPod Touch

The handbook of Britain's Special Air Service is now a rough-and-ready app for those who like to face Mother Nature head-on. The free app features excerpts from the book, with survival checklists and basic guides to finding water and navigating by the stars. The full app contains the entire guide plus 16 survival videos by an SAS instructor, an English-to-Morse Code generator, galleries of edible and inedible plants, and more.

TEXTBOOK CASES: Written by retired SAS soldier and instructor John "Lofty" Wiseman, the print version of the *SAS Survival Guide* became a standard reference for dealing with extreme encounters in the wild. The full SAS app includes the entire book, along with a survival quiz to see what you're made of, a sun compass, and a comprehensive first-aid section.

INTO THE WOODS: The *SAS Survival Guide* isn't one of those dusty old tomes of yesteryear. It shows you, in text, illustrations, photos, and videos, the equipment and skills you need to survive wilderness encounters, whether they're as tame as an annual Eagle Scout adventure in a national park or as fear-inducing as a bear that invites himself to dinner.

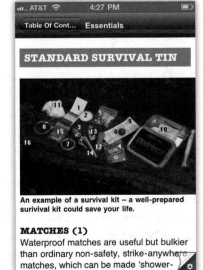

Best App for Bird-Watching

BirdsEye

$1.99 | $19.99 for full version
Version 1.2 | Birds in the Hand LLC
For all iPhones and the iPod Touch

Even if you know the difference between a Northern cardinal and a tufted titmouse, BirdsEye can open your eyes to hundreds of feathered friends. The app includes bird photos, profiles, audio clips of calls and cries, and maps of bird sightings, along with driving directions to see them. The Lite edition covers 135 common species, while the full version brings 847 North American birds home to roost on your iPhone or iPod Touch.

FIELD GUIDE: Tap the small red "+" dot in the corner of any photo to expand the image full-screen so you can see the bird's markings more clearly. BirdsEye's database has one or two recorded examples of most bird calls, so you can learn to identify each winged wonder by its sound as well as its plumage.

SPOT THE BIRDIE: If you're looking for a particular fowl, check BirdsEye's listings. The app collects regularly updated information that avid birders submit to the eBird database at the Cornell Lab of Ornithology. It presents that information in list form and on a map so you can find out where—and when—the bird was last seen.

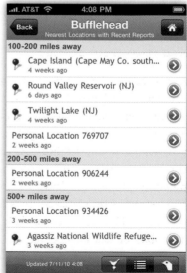

Best App for Sky-Watching

Star Walk
$2.99
Version 4.5 | Vito Technology Inc.
For all iPhones and the iPod Touch

Enhanced by ethereal music (that you can mute), this portable planetarium vividly depicts 9,000 stars, planets, and other heavenly bodies right on your screen. Raise an iPhone 3GS or 4 skyward, and the app's digital compass pinpoints you and displays a virtual version of the skyscape you see, complete with overlaid constellations and labels on heavenly bodies. As you move the iPhone, the star map shifts along with you.

THE DAILY PLANETS: Launch Star Walk and you see the rising and setting times for planets in the night sky. Tap the arrows in the top-right corner to see the schedule for a different date, or tap the ❌ button to move on to the stars.

THE SKY'S THE LIMIT: In Planetarium mode, Star Walk reveals the galaxy itself. It displays the constellations, planets, and stars of the part of the sky where you point your iPhone. Drag your finger across the screen to pan around the sky.

Best App for Gardening

GardenPilot

Free | $2.99 for full version
Version 3.0 | Scott Cissel
For all iPhones and the iPod Touch

When it comes to figuring out what to plant this year, GardenPilot serves as a handheld reference to plants, herbs, and vegetables available from mail-order houses like Burpee or from your local garden-supply store. While the free version of the app covers basic herbs and vegetables, the full version covers 13 types of vegetation (14,000 plants in all) with color photos that describe the plant's foliage, blooming season, light requirements, and more.

GREEN ZONE: GardenPilot's Navigator screen organizes plants, flowers, herbs, shrubs, and trees into categories. Tap a category to browse big color images of the plants, or tap Search to look for a plant by its common or Latin name. For articles about plants and procedures (raised-bed gardening, for example), tap Articles.

SEED CATALOG: When you find a plant or veggie you like, tap its thumbnail image to enlarge it to full-screen. To see its botanical name, sun and water requirements, and growth height, tap the Tag button (ⓘ). Tap the Buy Local button to find the plant/veggie at nearby grocery stores, or to buy the bulbs/seeds at a garden-supply store.

Best App for Weather Forecasts

WeatherBug
Free | $0.99 for full version
Version 1.4 | AWS Convergence Technologies
For all iPhones and the iPod Touch

You'll find plenty of great weather apps in the App Store, but Weather-Bug focuses less on flashy graphics and more on detailed descriptions of hourly weather conditions using info from a huge network of weather stations. The app has its share of visual goodies, too, like radar maps, videos, and live weather cameras. The freebie app serves up ads with your forecasts, but the paid edition replaces the ads with more maps and features.

INSTANT INFO: Before venturing outside, use WeatherBug to see if the forces of nature are with you. The app shows you the conditions at your current location, the forecast for the next hour or the next seven days, National Weather Service alerts, zoomable radar maps, and weather cams. Mark your favorite locations on the map with a pin, and tap the pin to see the conditions and temperature there.

Hurricane
$3.99
Version: 3.3 | Kitty Code LLC
For all iPhones and the iPod Touch

While those in non-coastal areas may not need it, the Hurricane app can be a lifesaver for people in storm-prone areas like the Gulf of Mexico. Beautifully designed to depict horrible weather, Hurricane provides animated satellite images, data from the National Hurricane Center, and tracking maps to highlight areas in danger as a storm approaches. The images for 5-day forecasts make it obvious when it's time to evacuate—or when the storm will blow on by.

Index

Numbers

A

B

Free Apps